Why Christian Faith Still Makes Sense

Acadia Studies in Bible and Theology

Craig A. Evans and Lee Martin McDonald, General Editors

The last two decades have witnessed dramatic developments in biblical and theological study. Full-time academics can scarcely keep up with fresh discoveries, recently published primary texts, ongoing archaeological work, new exegetical proposals, experiments in methods and hermeneutics, and innovative theological syntheses. For students and nonspecialists, these developments are confusing and daunting. What has been needed is a series of succinct studies that assess these issues and present their findings in a way that students, pastors, laity, and nonspecialists will find accessible and rewarding. Acadia Studies in Bible and Theology, sponsored by Acadia Divinity College in Wolfville, Nova Scotia, and in conjunction with the college's Hayward Lectureship, constitutes such a series.

The Hayward Lectureship has brought to Acadia many distinguished scholars of Bible and theology, such as Sir Robin Barbour, John Bright, Leander Keck, Helmut Koester, Richard Longenecker, Martin Marty, Jaroslav Pelikan, Ian Rennie, James Sanders, and Eduard Schweizer. The Acadia Studies in Bible and Theology series reflects this rich heritage.

These studies are designed to guide readers through the ever more complicated maze of critical, interpretative, and theological discussion taking place today. But these studies are not introductory in nature; nor are they mere surveys. Authored by leading authorities in the field, the Acadia Studies in Bible and Theology series offers critical assessments of the major issues that the church faces in the twenty-first century. Readers will gain the requisite orientation and fresh understanding of the important issues that will enable them to take part meaningfully in discussion and debate.

Why Christian Faith Still Makes Sense

A RESPONSE TO CONTEMPORARY CHALLENGES

C. STEPHEN EVANS

Baker Academic

a division of Baker Publishing Group
Grand Rapids, Michigan

Published by Baker Academic
a division of Baker Publishing Group
P.O. Box 6287, Grand Rapids, MI 49516-6287
www.bakeracademic.com

Printed in the United States of America

Library of Congress Cataloging-in-Publication Data is on file at the Library of Congress, Washington, DC.

ISBN 978-0-8010-9660-0

15   16   17   18   19   20   21   7   6   5   4   3   2   1

Contents

Preface

This book grew out of an invitation I received to give the Hayward Lectures at Acadia Divinity College at Acadia University in Wolfville, Nova Scotia, October 15–17, 2012. The general title of the lectures was "Christian Belief in the 21st Century: Responding to the New Atheism." Of course, the three lectures have been expanded to make a proper book, but some of the character of the book no doubt reflects its origins as a lecture series. In some ways, the subtitle of the lecture series is misleading. As readers of the book will quickly note, I do not engage very seriously with the leading "New Atheist" writers. This is primarily because I do not find the arguments and ideas of these writers worthy of serious refutation. In comparison with contemporary atheist philosophers of religion such as William Rowe, Paul Draper, and Evan Fales, whose writings constitute thoughtful and serious challenges to faith, the New Atheists show a lack of philosophical understanding and sophistication. (The exception to that claim is Daniel Dennett, who is a first-rate philosopher but who still reveals a lack of expertise in the philosophy of religion.)

Nevertheless, I think the subtitle is still accurate. I take it that the major complaint (though not the only one) of the New

Atheists about religion is that faith is intellectually baseless. In this book I try to give a clear case that belief in Christian faith still makes sense and thus answer that criticism. Although Christian faith requires the ability to stare down some of the intellectual fads and fashions of our age, it does not require the sacrifice of the mind. So the book answers a major charge the New Atheists make not by responding to their specific complaints but by showing how a thoughtful Christian might "give a reason for the hope" that faith embodies. In making a positive case the book transcends the criticisms of the New Atheists and thus can be read with interest by anyone wanting to explore the truth of faith questions. The other major complaint of the New Atheists is that religion "poisons everything" and is a net harm to society. On that score I am content to refer readers to other writers who are more competent to respond to that criticism than I am.

Some of the ideas in the first part of the book were developed in a more rigorous and lengthy form in my book *Natural Signs and Knowledge of God: A New Look at Theistic Arguments*. The germ of my approach goes back even further to *Why Believe? Reason and Mystery as Pointers to God*. However, I believe that in this work I have been able to say some of the things I have said before in new and clearer ways. The second half of the book, particularly the discussion of criteria for revelation, contains some ideas I have not discussed in print before. However, I believe it will be obvious how much I have profited from a lifetime of reading and study of Kierkegaard's work, so I claim no great originality for my approach. However, given Kierkegaard's forthright denunciation of apologetics, I dare not claim that this is a book he would have liked, however much it draws on his insights.

I must in conclusion express my deep gratitude to Craig Evans and the Acadia Divinity College faculty for the invitation to give the Hayward Lectures. I am honored to be included among the distinguished scholars who preceded me. The Acadia community welcomed my wife and me with such wonderful hospitality that this time will always be remembered fondly, not least for the chance to experience the beauty of Nova Scotia.

I must also thank Baylor University for a research leave during the spring semester of 2014 and Biola University for a research fellowship awarded by the Center for Christian Thought for the same semester. Although this book was not my primary project during that semester, the release from teaching my normal Baylor classes provided valuable time, and the congenial environment of the Center for Christian Thought at Biola provided the perfect milieu to bring this project to fruition. I must also thank my graduate research assistant, Matthew Wilson, who made a number of helpful suggestions and also tracked down some quotations and references for this book. I also wish to thank Maureen Ryan for compiling the index. Finally, I must thank my wife, Jan Evans, without whom I would accomplish nothing, for her wise advice, unwavering support, and steadfast love.

C. Stephen Evans
April 2014

Who Are the New Atheists, and What Are They Saying?

From the earliest periods of the Christian church, God has called some to defend the faith against the attacks of unbelievers. In the ancient world early Christians were variously accused of being atheists (because of their rejection of local gods), superstitious (because of their acceptance of miracles, such as the resurrection of Jesus), and subverters of the social order (because of their refusal to worship the emperor and their inclusion of people of all social classes in their communities). Such writers as Justin Martyr, Clement of Alexandria, and Origen responded to all these charges and more. Many apologists have taken 1 Peter 3:15 as providing a kind of charter for the apologetic enterprise: "Always be prepared to give an answer to everyone who asks you to give a reason for the hope that you have." Peter may not be referring directly to what has come to be known as apologetics, but this verse does seem to imply that Christian hope is not baseless or groundless. A person who possesses Christian faith can approach the world with an attitude of hope regardless of what transpires in this world, and this hope is one that is reasonable, at least from the perspective of faith. Recently, a number of writers, often collectively called "the New Atheists," have loudly claimed that Christian faith is anything but reasonable. What should the church say in response to such claims? I shall try to answer this question in this book. In this introductory chapter I must first say something about the New Atheists. Who are they? What exactly are their accusations against religious faith in general and Christian faith in particular?

The "Four Horsemen" of the New Atheists

A host of writers could be included under the label of the New Atheism, but I shall limit my discussion to four of the best-known writers: Richard Dawkins, Christopher Hitchens, Sam Harris, and Daniel Dennett, a quartet sometimes described as the "Four Horsemen" of the movement. (Though perhaps one should say that the Four Horsemen are now only a trio, since Christopher Hitchens passed away from pneumonia stemming from cancer in 2011.) Dawkins, an evolutionary biologist now at Oxford, first came to public attention with the publication of *The Selfish Gene* in 1976, a popular work in evolutionary biology that proposed that an organism should be thought of as merely a way that genes reproduce themselves.[1] Dawkins later argued in *The Blind Watchmaker* (1986) that the universe is fully intelligible without resort to any intelligent design or cause and in *The God Delusion* (2006) that religious belief is not only irrational but positively harmful.[2] Dawkins is unafraid to voice his contempt for biblical faith: "The God of the Old Testament is

---

1. Richard Dawkins, *The Selfish Gene*, 2nd ed. (Oxford: Oxford University Press, 1998).

2. Richard Dawkins, *The Blind Watchmaker: Why the Evidence of Evolution Reveals a Universe without Design* (New York: W. W. Norton, 1986) and *The God Delusion* (Boston: Houghton Mifflin, 2006).

arguably the most unpleasant character in all fiction: jealous and proud of it; a petty, unjust, unforgiving control-freak; a vindictive, bloodthirsty ethnic cleanser; a misogynistic, homophobic, racist, infanticidal, genocidal, filicidal, pestilential, megalomaniacal, sadomasochistic, capriciously malevolent bully."[3]

Christopher Hitchens, educated at Oxford, was a British leftist (Trotskyite initially) who made a living as a journalist, writing for *The Nation*, *The New Statesman*, and a variety of American publications, including *The Atlantic* and *Vanity Fair*. Besides his regular work as a journalist, Hitchens wrote a series of mostly biographical books, some on figures he admired (George Orwell, Thomas Paine, and Thomas Jefferson) and others on figures he detested (Henry Kissinger and Mother Teresa, no less). Hitchens acquired some notoriety by deserting his leftist friends and giving whole-hearted support to the American-led invasion of Iraq in 2003. However, even if he deviated from his leftist political views, he nonetheless remained consistent to the end in his vehement opposition to religious belief. *God Is Not Great: How Religion Poisons Everything* expresses his view that religion is not only false but pernicious, a cancer that right-thinking people should try to extirpate, though Hitchens is pessimistic that this is possible in the foreseeable future. Hitchens is probably even more quotable than Dawkins and is similarly unafraid to voice his outrage that religion persists in the contemporary world: "Religion has run out of justifications. Thanks to the telescope and the microscope, it no longer offers an explanation of anything important. Where once it used to be able, by its total command of a worldview, to *prevent* the emergence of rivals, it can now only impede and retard—or try to turn back—the measurable advances that we have made."[4]

3. Dawkins, *God Delusion*, 51.
4. Christopher Hitchens, *God Is Not Great: How Religion Poisons Everything* (New York: Twelve, 2007), 282.

Sam Harris received a PhD in neuroscience but is best known for his vociferous attacks on religious belief. His books include *The End of Faith* (2005) and *Letter to a Christian Nation* (2006), a short response to criticisms of the first book.[5] Harris has recently written *The Moral Landscape* (2010), in which he argues (naively) that ethical questions can and should be answered scientifically, and a short book entitled *Free Will* (2012).[6] Harris's attacks on religious belief, like those of Dawkins and Hitchens, do not focus solely on fundamentalism or extremist forms of religion. He thinks that even moderate forms of religious belief are destructive and harmful to our civilization: "We will see that the greatest problem confronting civilization is not merely religious extremism; it is the larger set of cultural and intellectual accommodations we have made to faith itself."[7]

The last of the "Four Horsemen" I shall briefly describe is Daniel Dennett, a philosopher at Tufts University best known for his work in the philosophy of mind and on free will, particularly with respect to the question of whether artificially constructed machines could ever be said to be conscious. Although Dennett's views in philosophy of mind, like all such views currently on offer, are controversial and hotly debated, he has won a reputation as an accomplished and influential philosopher in this area through such works as *Brainstorms* (1978),[8] *The Intentional Stance* (1987),[9] and *Consciousness Explained* (1991).[10] (Though I respect Dennett as a philosopher, I cannot resist

5. Sam Harris, *The End of Faith: Religion, Terror, and the Future of Reason* (New York: W. W. Norton, 2005) and *Letter to a Christian Nation* (New York: Alfred A. Knopf, 2006).

6. Sam Harris, *The Moral Landscape: How Science Can Determine Human Values* (New York: Free Press, 2010) and *Free Will* (New York: Free Press, 2012).

7. Harris, *End of Faith*, 45.

8. Daniel C. Dennett, *Brainstorms: Philosophical Essays on Mind and Psychology* (Montgomery, VT: Bradford, 1978).

9. Daniel C. Dennett, *The Intentional Stance* (Cambridge, MA: MIT Press, 1987).

10. Daniel C. Dennett, *Consciousness Explained* (Boston: Little, Brown, 1991).

passing on a standing joke among philosophers that Dennett should have called that last-mentioned book *Consciousness Explained Away*.) In 1995 Dennett shifted from narrow issues in the philosophy of mind to broader questions about a naturalistic worldview by defending the power of Darwinism to explain just about everything in *Darwin's Dangerous Idea*.[11] He moved toward explicit criticism of religion in *Breaking the Spell* (2006), which on the surface is simply a call for the scientific study of religion but (as the title implies) suggests that such study will break the hold that religion has on the minds and lives of people.[12] After the publication of *Breaking the Spell* Dennett participated in a memorable exchange with Alvin Plantinga, a distinguished Christian philosopher, and the exchange (including replies from each to the other) has been published as *Science and Religion: Are They Compatible?* (2011).[13]

The New Atheist Claims

What do these "Four Horsemen" have to say to us? What, if anything, is new about the New Atheism? In some respects, little is new in the attacks on religion mounted by these four thinkers. There are frequent denunciations of religion as outmoded and primitive and grand claims that religion is "unscientific." Religious beliefs are described as simply preposterous for a scientifically educated person; in fact, Harris claims that if the kinds of beliefs held by religious people were not widely shared, they would be regarded as evidence of mental illness. However, there is little in the way of detailed arguments to back up such

11. Daniel C. Dennett, *Darwin's Dangerous Idea: Evolution and the Meanings of Life* (New York: Touchstone, 1995).

12. Daniel C. Dennett, *Breaking the Spell: Religion as a Natural Phenomenon* (New York: Viking, 2006).

13. Daniel C. Dennett and Alvin Plantinga, *Science and Religion: Are They Compatible?* (Oxford: Oxford University Press, 2011).

grand claims, and in reality none of the Four Horsemen has any real competence in the philosophy of religion or (apparently) much familiarity with classical and contemporary debates in the field. I have privately heard from atheist philosophers of religion that they find the writings of the New Atheists somewhat embarrassing. In any case the assertions that religious beliefs are unsupported by evidence and have somehow been undermined by science have been stock claims made by atheists since at least the early nineteenth century. The idea that a naturalistic or materialistic worldview is somehow a more "scientific" view is practically a cliché.

There are, to be sure, a few novel arguments for the falsity of religious belief given by the New Atheists. A good example can be found in Richard Dawkins's claim that a God posited to explain the design of the natural order would be immensely improbable because "any God capable of designing anything would have to be complex enough to demand the same kind of explanation in his own right."[14] In effect Dawkins is arguing that postulating God explains nothing, since what is posited is just as much in need of explanation as what God is supposed to explain. Even worse, Dawkins thinks that postulating God to explain the natural order in this way would lead to an infinite regress of causes, presumably because we would need to postulate another God, equally complex, to explain God, and yet another God to explain God #2, and so on.[15]

It is an understatement to say that this argument fails to impress. First of all, even if Dawkins's argument were sound, it would not necessarily be damaging to the theist. Many theists believe that God is not affirmed on the basis of any kind of argument or inference, so even if the argument from design fails, this would not affect their belief. This is the view held by

14. Dawkins, *God Delusion*, 139.
15. Ibid., 109.

Alvin Plantinga and a group of philosophers called "Reformed epistemologists," whose views will be discussed later. However, even those who think that belief in God should be based on arguments may well think that there are other, better arguments than the argument from design, so the failure of this one argument is not necessarily a problem.

Another significant problem for Dawkins is that the key premise for his argument, which is his assumption that the cause of complex order must always be as complex as the order it causes, seems very weak. Why should one think this claim is true? It certainly is not obvious that some simple reality or event could not cause some very complex event. After all, one person assassinating an archduke is commonly said to be the cause of World War I, which is certainly a complex reality!

However, the most serious problem with Dawkins's argument is that it reveals a basic lack of understanding of what theologians mean when they talk about God. Anyone knowledgeable about the history of theology would know that one of the traditional attributes of God (going all the way back to Plotinus and Plato) is simplicity. Any being with parts, certainly any being with material parts, would not be God just because that being has parts. Dawkins's attempt to argue that an infinite series of explanations would be problematic actually mimics another classical argument *for* God's existence. This is the cosmological argument, which (in one of its versions) holds that one must postulate a simple, uncaused cause of the universe precisely because the universe consists of complex entities that require a cause. If one postulates another complex entity as that cause, then an infinite regress threatens. One can avoid such a regress only by postulating an ultimate cause that is not complex but simple, having no parts. Such a cause would be God, at least as many philosophers have understood God. Ironically, then, Dawkins's critique of the argument from design comes close to being another one of the classical arguments *for* God's existence. At least it includes key elements of such an argument. Most of the New Atheist criticisms of religious belief turn out to be familiar and not new at all; the genuinely new arguments (such as the one just examined) seem too weak to warrant a serious rebuttal.

There are, however, elements in the writings of the New Atheists that seem somewhat new. One is a brash confidence the New Atheists have in their antireligious claims and a willingness to assert them loudly and publicly. The New Atheists do not want to write articles for philosophy periodicals; they want to write best sellers that will command cultural attention. And they have been remarkably successful at this. Many bookshops now have a section of "New Atheist" titles that rival their religion section.

A second element in New Atheist writings that is at least relatively new is a conviction that religious beliefs are not only false and unreasonable but are ethically and socially harmful. Older atheists sometimes made such arguments but were often willing to concede that religious people had done good things as well. The New Atheists are absolutely convinced that many of the social ills that beset the twenty-first century can be traced to religion, including wars and violence of all kinds, sexism, and homophobia. They think that in the past some atheists have given religion too much credit for the good that happens in society. Those older atheists argued that although religion may produce social benefits (it cannot be denied that religious believers established the first universities and hospitals, for example), a person of intellectual integrity cannot be religious. The New Atheists are unwilling to concede any such benefits to religious belief. On their view, religion is not just intellectually groundless; it is positively harmful, both to the individual and to society, especially in the political realm. Furthermore, they think that this harmfulness is not merely something that stems from religious extremism or fanaticism. Rather, they argue that even religious moderates "provide protective coloration for their fanatical coreligionists."[16]

It is probably this second element that leads to the shrillness of the New Atheist polemics, and it leads to a third element, which may be the most novel aspect of their thinking: a questioning of the principle of religious tolerance. Most unbelievers in the past have accepted the idea of religious freedom, wanting only to ensure that the principle extends to unbelief as much as belief. The New Atheists think that religion is so irrational and so harmful to society that it may be something that should not be tolerated. While not willing to go so far as to propose some kind of atheist inquisition that would have power to punish religious believers, some of them are willing to consider whether restrictions should be put on the religious instruction of children. Hitchens, for example, provocatively asks, "Is religion child abuse?" and implies in the chapter of that title that it is that and worse.[17] He also affirms that "if religious instruction were not allowed until the child attains the age of reason, we would live in a quite different world."[18] There is a general view among the New Atheists that religious beliefs are harmful enough that they deserve no special protections or privileged status in society.

Here we see a genuine reversal in thinking. Prior to the development in modern times of societies tolerant of religious beliefs, it was often thought that the lack of religious faith was something so harmful to society (and to the individuals who lacked faith) that it should not be tolerated. As a result, people of good will and with good motives wound up persecuting religious dissenters, a practice now generally believed, in European

16. Dennett, *Breaking the Spell*, 301. Dennett here echoes and applauds a theme in Sam Harris's *End of Faith*.
17. Hitchens, *God Is Not Great*, 217–28.
18. Ibid., 220.

and North American countries at least, to be profoundly wrong. The New Atheists seem to think that the harmfulness of religious beliefs may, in a similar way, justify policies of intolerance toward religion. We have thus gone from intolerance of unbelief to serious discussion of (or outright support for) policies that at least border on intolerance of belief.

How Should Christians Respond?

A comprehensive response to the New Atheism should touch on all of the issues I have just mentioned, and much good work has been done toward this end. For example, the claim that Christian belief is incompatible with science has been examined and found wanting by philosophers such as Alvin Plantinga as well as scientists such as physicist John Polkinghorne and biologist Francis Collins.[19] The charge that religious belief in general, and Christian belief in particular, has been and continues to be ethically destructive also deserves a serious reply. Of course, Christians should honestly admit that the Christian church, as well as many individual Christians, has often exhibited moral failure, something that the Christian doctrine of sin implies should not be surprising to us. However, the narrative provided by the New Atheists on the moral effects of Christian belief, both in the past and today, is one-sided and inaccurate. They focus on the less-than-adequate ways Christians have expressed their faith while ignoring or minimizing the incredible ways Christian love and compassion have changed society for the good.

Good work has been done in this area as well. Distinguished philosopher Nicholas Wolterstorff, for example, has argued

---

19. See Alvin Plantinga's recent *Where the Conflict Really Lies: Science, Religion, and Naturalism* (Oxford: Oxford University Press, 2011). Also see John Polkinghorne, *Belief in God in an Age of Science* (New Haven: Yale University Press, 1998), and Francis Collins, *The Language of God: A Scientist Presents Evidence for Belief* (New York: Free Press, 2006).

convincingly that the important doctrine of human rights historically stemmed from biblical faith and that even today there is no adequate replacement for a religious vision of human nature as a basis for human rights.[20] Distinguished historian Jeffrey Burton Russell has answered many of the "viral" lies and legends found in New Atheist writings in his book *Exposing Myths about Christianity*.[21] Rodney Stark, in *The Victory of Reason: How Christianity Led to Freedom, Capitalism, and Western Success*,[22] presents a powerful answer to the New Atheist attack. Stark's narrative may at times be a bit unbalanced on the other side in his defense of Christian belief, but he makes a strong case that the success of science and the development of political freedom, both developments that are highly prized by the New Atheists, were the outgrowth of a religious view rather than something made possible by secularization.

Given the unoriginality of the New Atheists' intellectual attacks, one might well think that the most important area of response lies in this clearing of the historical air by reexamining the historical and ethical implications of faith. This kind of response is indeed extremely important. The New Testament says that "by their fruits you shall know them," and so the charge that Christian faith leads only to bad fruit must be confronted, even while the church's mistakes are honestly admitted and repented of. However, I believe that it is also important to confront the New Atheism on basic intellectual grounds. A failure to clearly articulate why reasonable people can believe that Christian faith is true plays right into the hands of anti-theists.

20. See Nicholas Wolterstorff, *Justice: Rights and Wrongs* (Princeton: Princeton University Press, 2008).

21. Jeffrey Burton Russell, *Exposing Myths about Christianity: A Guide to Answering 145 Viral Lies and Legends* (Downers Grove, IL: InterVarsity, 2012).

22. Rodney Stark, *The Victory of Reason: How Christianity Led to Freedom, Capitalism, and Western Success* (New York: Random House, 2005).

It is true that the New Atheists think that religious believers have many more faults than being intellectually unreasonable; on their view religious beliefs are a prime source of violence and suffering in today's world. However, since the New Atheists see themselves as committed to reason, particularly as exercised through science, the first sin of religious believers in their eyes is to not follow reason. Presumably, if the New Atheists were convinced that some set of religious beliefs was solidly grounded in reason, and we therefore had strong evidence of the truth of those beliefs, then they would affirm that all of us would be right to believe those claims regardless of any untoward ethical implications the beliefs might have. (At least this is what they ought to say, as people who claim to be committed to following reason and evidence.)

It is of course the case that a central belief of Christianity, and of Judaism and Islam, is the existence of God, an all-perfect, all-powerful, all-knowing being who is responsible for the existence of everything in the universe. The central importance of belief in God can be seen simply by looking at the titles of the New Atheists' books, which include *The God Delusion*, *God Is Not Great* (which argues for the nonexistence of God rather than simply his lack of goodness), and *The Blind Watchmaker* (which puts in place of a personal creator God a blind, random, natural process). The first part of a response to the New Atheists requires facing the question of whether belief in God makes sense in the contemporary world. Does reasonable belief in God require "proofs" or arguments? In the next chapter I shall try to show that although belief in God can be reasonable without the support of arguments, there are strong reasons for belief in God.

2

The Value of Natural Theology

Traditionally, many Christian theologians and philosophers have responded to the charge that belief in God is unjustified by engaging in *natural theology*, the attempt to determine what can be known about God and God's attributes simply by appealing to natural human reason and experience. The first elements of natural theology usually consist of offering arguments or pointing to some kind of evidence that is generally accessible to humans and supports belief in God. An influential and popular form of natural theology was presented in the mid-twentieth century by C. S. Lewis in *Mere Christianity*.[1] Defenders of natural theology can still be found, particularly among Christian philosophers, and I will say more about this below. However, I think it is fair to say that natural theology is not prominent in the work of contemporary theologians, and even that many theologians, particularly Protestants, view natural theology with some suspicion.

1. C. S. Lewis, *Mere Christianity* (London: Collins, 1952).

I shall try in this chapter to address the reasons for this suspicion and make a positive case for a kind of natural theology. In this chapter I have three goals. First, I want to show the value of natural theology. I think that natural theology has a kind of value that its critics have overlooked and that can be recognized even by those critics. Second, I want to discuss the question of whether there is a "burden of proof" that must be shouldered by the natural theologian. Finally, I want to say something about the kind of evidence that the natural theologian should be expected to give, the kind of evidence that one would expect there to be if God does in fact exist.

The first thing worth noting is that this silence on the part of theologians has given the New Atheists a rhetorical advantage. One theme New Atheists constantly hammer on is that religion has no rational basis; it is something based on "faith," which they characterize simply as believing without evidence. Richard Dawkins recounts with some contempt a conference with theologians he participated in at Cambridge, at which he claims his argument for atheism met with no rational response: "The theologians of my Cambridge encounter were *defining* themselves into an epistemological Safe Zone where rational argument could not reach them."[2] The lack of a public voice that clearly defends the reasonableness of belief in God makes it appear that such belief has no reasonable ground. This may explain why the New Atheists actually spend so little time engaging the case for religious belief. They think that no serious case can be made, since religious belief depends on "faith." Hitchens thus declares that "what can be asserted without evidence can also be dismissed without evidence."[3]

It is, I think, fairly clear that the New Atheists, by and large, are "evidentialists" in their epistemology. Evidentialists hold

2. Dawkins, *God Delusion*, 154.
3. Hitchens, *God Is Not Great*, 150.

that beliefs that are rationally justified must be based on evidence, and in the case of religious beliefs the New Atheists are sure that the evidence is inadequate (or even nonexistent). How should Christians respond to this charge? One possibility is to attack evidentialism. Those Christian philosophers known as "Reformed epistemologists" are inspired by John Calvin's claim that belief in God is produced by a *sensus divinitatis*, a natural faculty that God has given humans that produces belief in God. Belief in God that is the product of such a faculty can be *properly basic*, not based on any kind of argument or inference from any fact, according to this line of thought.[4]

The most prominent defender of Reformed epistemology is Alvin Plantinga, who has developed a formidable account of human knowledge to support his arguments about religious belief. According to Reformed epistemology, belief in God can be reasonable even if the believer has no arguments or propositional evidence on which the belief is based. Plantinga, like many epistemologists, accepts a version of "foundationalism." Foundationalists agree that some of our beliefs are based on other beliefs. For example, I believe the computer monitor I am looking at was made by Acer, but I believe that is true because I perceive the word "Acer" at the bottom of the monitor and believe that the Acer company puts its name on its products. Not all of our beliefs can be based on other beliefs, however, since this would mean that I would need an infinite number of beliefs in order to have any beliefs at all. In the example just given, my belief that the word "Acer" is on the monitor in front of me is not based on any other beliefs. It is something I perceive directly. That belief is, for me at this moment, basic or foundational.

Every foundationalist will therefore admit that it is reasonable to hold some beliefs that are basic or foundational in character.

---

4. For the classic account of this view, see Alvin Plantinga, *Warranted Christian Belief* (New York: Oxford University Press, 2000), particularly 167–98.

Obviously these beliefs will not require any argument or proof, since, if they were the result of an inference, they would not be basic. Reformed epistemologists argue that belief in God can be among our basic beliefs. If they are correct, then natural theology that consists of *arguments* for God's existence will not be necessary for reasonable belief in God.

I count myself a defender of Reformed epistemology. I believe its central contentions are correct, and I shall later say something about why this is so and how it can be useful in responding to the New Atheism. However, Reformed epistemology should not be the whole of our response to the New Atheism. After all, to say that belief in God *can* be reasonable without argument or propositional evidence does not imply that there *are* no good arguments or that powerful evidence cannot be given. It is quite consistent to hold that an evidential argument can be given for a belief even if that belief would be reasonable without that argument. So Reformed epistemology does not rule out the possibility of giving arguments for God's existence.

Even if we do not think we can give arguments for God's existence, we might still want to affirm that belief in God is based on evidence of a sort. Here we must think carefully about what we mean by "evidence." When the Reformed epistemologist argues that belief in God can be reasonable without evidence, he is using the term "evidence" to mean *propositional* evidence. The idea is that belief in God does not have to be based on other propositional beliefs or be arrived at through some process of inference. However, in daily life we often use the term "evidence" to refer to things other than propositions. A police officer may regard fingerprints collected at a crime scene as evidence. Experiences can also function as evidence; when I taste the sweetness of a soda, I may take the sweetness as evidence that the soda contains sugar. (Of course, evidence is not always conclusive; the soda might contain an artificial sweetener rather than sugar.) Neither fingerprints nor experiences are propositions, although they certainly can be described propositionally. Hence, even those who affirm that belief in God does not require propositional evidence might hold that we have nonpropositional evidence for God's reality.

If we simply affirm that belief in God can be reasonable without evidence (and say no more), this will look, especially to many laypeople incapable of understanding the subtle epistemology that underlies Reformed epistemology, like a confirmation of the New Atheists' claim that there is no evidence for belief in God. And that would be a false impression.

Critics of Natural Theology and "Two-Stage Apologetics"

Arguments for God's existence have often been understood as offering the first element of what I have elsewhere called a "two-stage apologetic."[5] The first stage consists of arguments or reasons to believe in God, with the second stage consisting of arguments or reasons to believe that God has revealed himself particularly in the history of Israel, in Jesus of Nazareth, and through the Scriptures that Christians believe to be inspired by God. This strategy can be seen in the work of many thinkers, from medieval philosophers such as Thomas Aquinas right through to C. S. Lewis and Richard Swinburne in the twentieth century.[6]

Despite the pedigree of this tradition, natural theology arguments have not been prominent among contemporary defenders of Christianity in the last century or so, especially among Protestant Christians. The reasons for this are complex. One is the widespread impression that the arguments of natural theology

---

5. See my *The Historical Christ and the Jesus of Faith: The Incarnational Narrative as History* (Oxford: Oxford University Press, 1996), 233–37.

6. See C. S. Lewis, *Mere Christianity* and *Miracles* (San Francisco: HarperOne, 2001). Also see Richard Swinburne, *The Christian God* (Oxford: Oxford University Press, 1994).

were dealt a fatal blow by the Enlightenment philosophers David Hume and Immanuel Kant. Of course, if the arguments are not good arguments, Christians will have to rely on something else. I suspect that some theologians, particularly those in the liberal camp, have thought something like this. In my view, however, the arguments from Hume and Kant that are alleged to be devastating are far from decisive. Oddly, one often finds theologians accepting the conclusions of Hume and Kant about natural theology while rejecting the epistemological stance on which those conclusions are based.

However, there are certainly other reasons for the decline in natural theology among Protestant theologians. One is the widespread suspicion that natural theology somehow undercuts or undermines the centrality of God's self-revelation as the primary means whereby humans can come to know God. There is little doubt that the towering influence of twentieth-century theologian Karl Barth has been very strong at this point.[7] I am far from being a Barth scholar, but I believe Barth had a number of distinct reasons to worry about natural theology, and I am sympathetic to some of them. One worry is that natural theology can lead to a kind of idolatry. If God is transcendent and "wholly other" to humans, then one might think that any knowledge of God we can come up with on our own will fail to do justice to God's transcendence. Indeed, it seems possible that we will "create God in our image," giving a kind of confirmation of the nineteenth-century German philosopher Ludwig Feuerbach's criticism of religion as a "projection" onto an imaginary world of what humans themselves yearn to become. (Feuerbach is famous for the claim that "all theology is anthropology.") Barth believed

---

7. In 1934 Barth published *Nein! Antwort an Emil Brunner* [No! An Answer to Emil Brunner], in which he argued that the syncretism and anti-Semitism linked to Christianity in Nazi Germany were rooted in natural theology. For an English translation see *Natural Theology: Comprising "Nature and Grace" and the Reply "No,"* ed. G. Bles (London: Centenary, 1946).

that to avoid this danger, any adequate knowledge of God must come from God's self-revelation rather than natural theology.

Recently, Christian philosopher Paul Moser has also criticized attempts to argue for God's existence in the traditional way. On Moser's view, such arguments at best lead to "thin theism," a set of beliefs about abstract metaphysical claims. However, Moser argues that thin theism is of no religious value. If there is a God, then the crucial issue is our status before God. God is not interested merely in our knowing such abstract propositions as "God exists." Rather, God wants us to know *him* and to acquire a proper relation to God. A genuine knowledge of God would be gained through a process in which we come to understand our moral and volitional status in relation to God and God's authority.

Traditional theistic arguments based on "spectator evidence"—evidence that can be had without any spiritual transformation on our part—do not serve such ends. So Moser thinks we must come to know God by being open to the experience of God and God's self-revelation.[8] Natural theology is a mistake. It gives the appearance that the evidence for God is weak, but that is because it is looking for the wrong kind of evidence. Genuine knowledge of God must be grounded in a full-fledged encounter with God's self-revelation where we must come to know God as Lord, which is how God wishes us to know him.

Natural Theology as Support for "Anti-naturalism"

Barth and Moser (and others saying similar things) express important insights. However, I believe we can accept their concerns

---

8. For Moser's own account of his views, see "Death, Dying, and the Hiddenness of God," in *The Philosophy of Religion Reader*, ed. Chad Meister (London: Routledge, 2008), 613–24; and "Cognitive Idolatry and Divine Hiding," in *Divine Hiddenness*, ed. D. Howard-Snyder and Paul Moser (New York: Cambridge University Press, 2002), 120–48. Also see idem, *The Elusive God: Reorienting Religious Epistemology* (Cambridge: Cambridge University Press, 2008).

as valid yet still see an important role for natural theology in responding to the New Atheism. The key is to see natural theology not as providing us with an adequate, positive knowledge of God but as supporting what I like to call "anti-naturalism." Roughly, by "anti-naturalism" I mean a stance in which one recognizes the problems with a naturalistic worldview that affirms the physical universe as the whole of reality. Anti-naturalists are open to the possibility that there is something or someone beyond nature, even if there is no clear knowledge of what that transcendent reality might be like.

Suppose that one agrees with the criticisms of Barth and Moser directed against natural theology. What follows from this for one who is not (yet) a religious believer? Does it mean that if I have not turned to God in faith by hearing and responding to his Word, or have not sought God by being open to his authority and correction, then the most reasonable view of the universe and our place in it would be a naturalistic view? Should a reasonable nonbeliever be an atheist? I think the answer to these questions is a resounding "no." To put things more plainly, I want to claim that a naturalistic view of reality itself suffers from deep problems. There are more things in heaven and earth than a naturalist can reasonably make sense of, and even someone who is not a full-fledged religious believer can understand the difficulties with naturalism.

I propose, then, that we reconceive natural theology as a defense of anti-naturalism. Many of the arguments of traditional natural theology point to aspects of the natural world that naturalism cannot fully explain. There are elements in nature that point beyond nature. My own term for these elements is "natural signs." Even if these natural signs do not give us genuine knowledge of God, they help us see that the natural world points beyond itself toward a profound mystery. Natural theology articulates questions that a reasonable person ought to ask. Even if the natural theologian cannot answer those questions satisfactorily, the questions point us toward the kind of answers that Barth and Moser want us to seek. To put things as simply as possible, I deny that naturalism is necessarily the most reasonable view of reality to take, even if one is not already a Christian believer.

To see how natural theology can help, one must have a clear understanding of the epistemic situation that confronts someone who is thinking about the merits of naturalism vis-à-vis its rivals. In particular one must have a clear view of where the burden of proof lies in relation to these questions and also what kind of evidence for God one would expect there to be if God exists and created the natural universe. I shall turn first to the issue of burden of proof.

Is God like the Loch Ness Monster? Naturalism and the Burden of Proof

It is clear that most atheists think that the burden of proof in relation to God lies with the religious believer. This assumption was articulated and defended by Antony Flew in his well-known essay "The Presumption of Atheism," in which he argued that atheism is the default position intellectually and that one should not be a theist without strong evidence.[9] Belief in God is intellectually risky, while naturalism is safe ground. This assumption seems right to many atheists because they think of God as "one more thing" in the universe. Theists and naturalists agree that

9. See Antony Flew, *The Presumption of Atheism and Other Essays on God, Freedom, and Immortality* (London: Pemberton, 1976). Interestingly, though Flew never changed his commitment to the need for evidence, he did toward the end of his life change his views about God, adopting a deistic view on the basis of a "fine-tuning" argument from the natural universe. See Antony Flew and Roy Abraham Varghese, *There Is a God: How the World's Most Notorious Atheist Changed His Mind* (New York: HarperCollins, 2008).

the universe contains dogs and cats, lions and tigers, trees and rocks. If they are scientifically sophisticated, perhaps they also agree about electrons, quarks, and black holes. However, the naturalist thinks that the traditional theist goes beyond this safe common ground and believes in one additional, strange entity, namely, God. Believing in God is like believing in the Loch Ness monster or the Yeti. Surely, one might think the person who believes in the Loch Ness monster bears a burden of proof that the skeptic about such things does not shoulder. If God is, like the Loch Ness monster, simply one more entity in the universe, then the religious believer bears a similar burden of proof.

However, this way of thinking about the issue is completely wrongheaded. On the traditional theistic conception of God, God is not simply another entity within the natural order, on a par with other entities. To believe in God is to believe the universe has a certain character; to disbelieve in God is to believe the universe lacks that character and has a very different character. The person who believes in God holds that each and every thing that exists, other than God, exists because of God and God's creative activity. The universe that God has made was created for a purpose, and part of that purpose is a contest between good and evil, a contest in which the character of the universe gives assurance that the good will ultimately win.

The naturalist, in sharp contrast, believes that each and every thing that exists as part of the natural order lacks this characteristic of existing because of God's creative activity. Instead, all these things exist "on their own," so to speak. One might say that for the naturalist, the universe is a brute fact. There is no reason or purpose behind the existence of the universe as a whole or the individual entities that compose it. Furthermore, we have no reason at all to think that good will win over evil or even that the contest between good and evil is a significant one. The theist and the naturalist do not just disagree about

God; they disagree about the character of everything that exists. Each is committed to a worldview that includes a perspective on what is ultimately real.

It is, I think, appropriate for the believer in God to consider what reasons the believer has for holding that the universe has the character that it does. But it is equally reasonable for the naturalist to reflect on the evidence for the truth of the naturalistic worldview. Moreover, it is by no means clear that the naturalistic worldview is somehow safer or less risky than a theistic worldview. No special burden of proof lies on the theist.

Many of the New Atheists, and many naturalists in general, fail to see this because they confuse a commitment to naturalism, which is a metaphysical view, with a commitment to natural science. Somehow, they believe, naturalism is supported by science, and one commonly hears a naturalistic worldview described as a "scientific worldview." However, the theist and the atheist do not, qua theist and atheist, disagree about any scientific questions at all. The question of naturalism is a question about whether nature is all there is.

Science, as currently understood, is an attempt to gain knowledge of the natural world. However, science by its very nature is not fit to investigate whether there is more to reality than the natural world investigated by science. The theist and the atheist can both agree that there are scientific laws that describe the behavior of the natural world. The theist believes those laws hold because of God's creative activity; the atheist can give no such explanation. But there are no scientific experiments that can decide the question of whether the natural world is all there is. Such questions are philosophical in nature.

As is the case with most philosophical questions, it is not possible to prove beyond doubt that one answer to such a question is correct, if we mean by a "proof" an argument that no reasonable person could doubt. In that sense God's existence cannot be proved. But it is equally true that in that sense of proof, naturalism cannot be proven to be the correct metaphysical picture of things. Proof in this sense is an unrealistic ideal for both the theist and the atheist. What is reasonable, however, is to ask ourselves which of these rival worldviews makes the most sense, taking into account all that we know. The question I now want to pose is, what kind of evidence should we expect to find if God does exist?

The Pascalian Constraints on Knowledge of God

Even the atheist can recognize that it is reasonable to consider the existence of God as a hypothesis (understanding the content of the hypothesis to be a claim about the character of reality as a whole and not just about God as "one more thing"). As is the case with any hypothesis, we can consider what consequences we would expect if that hypothesis is true. If we assume that God exists and has created human persons so that they can enjoy a relationship with God, then it is surely reasonable to assume that a knowledge of God would be possible for humans and that the grounds of that knowledge would be generally accessible. One would not think that the knowledge of God would require great philosophical learning or scientific sophistication; it would be exceedingly odd if someone had to be a theoretical physicist or have a PhD in philosophy in order to come to know God. Rather, one would expect that a knowledge of God would be generally available to ordinary people. If there is evidence of God's reality, we would expect that evidence to be fairly pervasive and easy to recognize. I call the claim that evidence for God would be widely available the "Wide Accessibility Principle."[10]

10. See my *Natural Signs and Knowledge of God* (Oxford: Oxford University Press, 2010), 12–15, 37–38, for a more extended discussion and defense of this principle.

However, Christian theology has generally assumed that God desires humans not just to have a relationship with him but to have a relationship of a certain kind. God desires humans to serve him freely, motivated by love of God's goodness, not out of coercion or fear. Given God's omnipotence and omniscience, if God's reality were too obvious it would create difficulties for this goal, for it would be the height of foolishness for even a self-centered being to oppose a being who is omnipotent and omniscient.

There is an old joke that goes like this: "Question: What do you give a six-hundred-pound gorilla in your living room to eat? Answer: Whatever he wants." An omnipotent, omniscient God, if his reality were too obvious, would be, like the gorilla, impossible to ignore. It thus seems plausible to assume that, though the evidence for God would be widely available and easily accessible, it would also be the kind of evidence that a person who wished to do so could dismiss or reject. We might thus expect the evidence to have a degree of ambiguity, to be such that it could be reinterpreted or explained away by those who do not wish to believe in God, or who perhaps have been taught to think this way by those who do not believe in God. The evidence would then be easily resistible, even though widely available, and I call this second constraint on the evidence for God the "Easy Resistibility Principle."[11]

Both of these principles are strongly suggested by some remarks made by Blaise Pascal in his *Pensées*.

> If he had wished to overcome the obstinacy of the most hardened, he could have done so by revealing himself to them so plainly that they could not doubt the truth of his essence. . . . It was therefore not right that he should appear in a manner manifestly divine and absolutely capable of convincing all men, but neither was it right that his coming should be so hidden

11. Again, see my *Natural Signs and Knowledge of God*, 15–17, 157–60.

that he could not be recognized by those who sincerely sought him. . . . Thus wishing to appear openly to those who seek him with all their heart and hidden from those who shun him with all their heart, he has qualified our knowledge of him by giving signs which can be seen by those who seek him and not by those who do not. "There is enough light for those who desire only to see and enough darkness for those of a contrary disposition."[12]

Pascal is likely thinking of the knowledge of the incarnate Christ in this passage rather than natural knowledge of God, but it is surely in the spirit of his thought to apply the same concerns to the latter. I therefore think it is appropriate to describe the Wide Accessibility Principle and the Easy Resistibility Principle as the two "Pascalian constraints" on evidence for God's existence.

Natural Theology and Anti-naturalism

One might wonder how natural theology conceived as support for anti-naturalism can be helpful in gaining knowledge of God. After all, anti-naturalism, as I have described it, does not necessarily include belief in God at all but may consist only of a vague sense that there is something beyond the natural order. Critics of natural theology, both religious and antireligious, sometimes say something similar by arguing that natural theology arguments at best lead to an abstract "philosophical god" rather than the God of the Bible.

This criticism is confused. True, natural theology does not give a reliable, precise knowledge of the biblical God. Historically, the "signs" that point beyond the natural world have often led to polytheism as well as a great variety of other beliefs about God or gods. As soon as we understand that the Easy Resistibility Principle holds and, thus, that the evidence God provides for

12. Blaise Pascal, *Pensées* (New York: E. P. Dutton, 1958), 118.

himself is somewhat unclear and ambiguous, then this result is inevitable.

In my view, this is not a problem, because it is not the purpose of natural theology to give us precise, reliable knowledge of God. Its purpose is to help us see the inadequacies of naturalism and to open us to the possibility that there is something beyond nature. The fact that it does not give us a clear knowledge of this reality should fill us with a desire to know more and give us an openness to the possibility of a fuller revelation. If there is a God who wants us to enjoy a relation with him, then we might expect him to provide such a revelation. Natural theology does not replace a full, special self-revelation of God; it makes us open to the possibility of such a revelation.

Conclusion

To do natural theology, we must get three things right. First, we must have a correct view of the goal of natural theology, construing it primarily as a defense of anti-naturalism rather than as giving us substantive, positive knowledge of God. Second, we must have the right view of where the burden of proof lies, recognizing that there is no "presumption of atheism" but that all rival worldviews are accountable to reason. Finally, we must have the right view of the kind of evidence needed and the reasonableness of seeking it. In the next chapter I shall try to show that there are indeed natural signs of God that God has placed in the natural world and in human experience. These signs satisfy the Wide Accessibility Principle as well as the Easy Resistibility Principle while making it possible to achieve the goals of natural theology, giving us reason to look for a special, fuller revelation from God.

3

The Concept of a Natural Sign for God

In the last chapter I argued that it was important to challenge the New Atheists' claim that there is no evidence for the reality of God. To do this we need a realistic view of the goals of natural theology arguments. We also need to recognize that there is no "presumption of atheism" but that the burden of proof lies equally on the rival worldviews of theism and naturalism. Finally, we need to have the right understanding of what kind of evidence is needed and might be possible. The evidence, I argued, should meet two Pascalian constraints: the Wide Accessibility Principle and the Easy Resistibility Principle.

We also saw that Pascal uses the term "signs" for the kind of evidence that meets these two constraints, and he was right to do so. On the one hand, signs can be evident and easy to grasp. Even children can read road signs. On the other hand, signs have to be interpreted, and it is possible to misinterpret them, as travel in a foreign country can teach a person. Signs can also be ignored. So signs can fail to achieve their intended purpose in a number of ways, both by being ignored and by being misread. Both cases admit of what we might call innocent mistakes as well as more willful problems. Sometimes someone just misses a sign, and sometimes people have not learned how to read or interpret a sign. But there are also cases where someone intentionally ignores a sign or refuses to admit what the sign means. (We might think here of the case of a stereotypical male driver who does not want to admit any need for help!) Hence, the concept of a sign seems a promising one to employ to understand how a natural knowledge of God might be possible. However, what might it mean to speak of a *natural* sign? And what would a natural sign for God be like?

Thomas Reid's Concept of a Natural Sign

Natural signs are signs whose meaning is not conventionally established, in contrast to human highway signs. Rather, humans have a natural disposition to read a natural sign in a certain way. I borrow the term "natural sign" from the Scottish Enlightenment philosopher Thomas Reid, who uses it in his theory of perception. My concept of a natural sign for God, which I shall call a "theistic natural sign," is modeled on his concept of a perceptual natural sign.[1] Reid holds that perception of the world is made possible by sensations we receive from that world, and he calls those sensations natural signs. However, unlike many other modern philosophers who attempted to show how we could infer the existence of the perceived world by reasoning from the inner sensations we have awareness of directly, Reid holds that in the typical case our perception of the external world is psychologically direct. We do not perceive sensations and infer that there is a world. We perceive the world by way of sensations.

1. For a more developed account of Reid's concept of a natural sign, see my *Natural Signs and Knowledge of God*, 26–34.

When we see green grass, for example, we do not normally *infer* the existence of the grass. We do *not* rely on arguments such as, "I am having the kind of sensations one would expect to have if there were green grass in front of me. So there is probably green grass in front of me." We do not perform any act of inference or reasoning at all. Rather, we simply have the sensations and form the belief that we are looking at grass, assuming we are paying attention in the right way and that we know what grass is. It might be *possible* to reason from sensations to the things we perceive by them (although Reid is doubtful that it is); to do that we would need to direct our attention to the sign itself rather than, as is normally the case, to what we perceive by way of the sign. But even if it is possible to reason from the sign to what is perceived by the sign, it is not necessary in normal cases.

Reid thinks that some of the natural signs we see are "original," in the sense that we do not need to be taught their meaning. An example is the sensation of hardness we have when we press against a solid object. In this case we are "hardwired," so to speak, to form the belief that the object is solid. It is important to realize that there is no resemblance between the sensation we have and the quality of the object we come to recognize by means of the sensation. The feeling of hardness is not itself hard, and so the sensation is not a "copy" or representation of the hard object. Another example of original natural signs would include facial expressions; it appears that even infants naturally respond to smiles with smiles of their own and perceive angry facial expressions as threatening.

However, most natural signs are not original but learned. We experience the smell of a lemon on several occasions and develop the ability to recognize a lemon just from that smell. Even though the meaning of the sign is learned in the latter case, the recognition of the lemon is still psychologically direct and requires no inference or reasoning. Learned natural signs are in one sense just as natural as original natural signs, because they are the product of our natural faculties functioning in a proper manner.

I shall argue that the natural signs for God are signs in this learned sense. This is important because it means that some people might be aware of the signs but fail to realize that the signs point to God, simply because they have not learned their meaning. Here there could be two types of cases, one type innocent and one type willful. Some people might simply have not made the connections, or perhaps they just have not been taught to make them. Another innocent example might be a simple mistake in interpretation that is not willful. However, other people might willfully ignore the sign or intentionally misinterpret it.

What is necessary for a natural sign to be a natural sign? Reid thinks that we need at least three things. First, we need a causal connection between the sign and what the sign signifies so that the sign can be a reliable indicator of what it signifies. Second, in order for a sign to be a sign, it must have the purpose or function of being a sign. For Reid, sensations are natural signs because they are designed by God to give us perceptual knowledge. Third, for a sign to be a *natural* sign, there must be a native tendency on the part of those who receive the signs to respond appropriately by "reading" the sign correctly.

To say that such a tendency is native or original does not mean that it does not require some kind of learning to be activated. Here we might think of the case of mathematics. People have a natural disposition to think mathematically. For example, they have a natural tendency to realize that if they add two bananas to the two bananas they already have, they will have four bananas. However, this natural mathematical ability is not present from birth, and it requires the right kind of nurturing to be activated. One might even imagine some isolated culture that is totally lacking in the concept of a number, and perhaps people brought up in that culture lack the ability to see that two things added to two things makes four things. Still, mathematical knowledge is not purely the result of culture, and this can be seen by the fact that basic mathematical truths are recognized by humans in virtually every culture. People in different cultures have independently come to recognize many of the same mathematical truths, in some cases even advanced and complicated truths.

Theistic Natural Signs and the *Sensus Divinitatis*

It is not difficult to see that all of these conditions could easily be met by signs that God has given of his reality. First, if God exists and is the creator of all things, then there will always be a causal connection between God and the signs, because God is the cause of the existence of everything other than himself. Second, it is quite conceivable that God has made certain features of the natural world, such as beautiful sunsets or magnificent ocean or mountain vistas, with the intention that those features be signs that point to him. Third, God could easily give humans a natural tendency to respond to those signs by forming belief in God or gods. Note that it makes no difference *how* God might instill this natural disposition.

Some religious believers think that God created humans by a direct act and not from any previous form of life. Clearly, in that case God could have put into humans any disposition he wished. However, the same would be true if God created humans through some evolutionary process. Some people might believe that if God uses an evolutionary process, then he would not be "in control" and could not guarantee that humans would have any specific qualities. However, this is a mistake. Any evolutionary process by which humans might have come into existence would depend on the laws of nature and on what material things exist. However, if God exists and is the creator of the world, then he is responsible both for the existence of the natural world and for the natural laws that govern the events of that world. Nothing can ever be out of his control, though he might choose to allow creatures to have free will to disobey his commands. So there is no reason why God could not use an evolutionary process to instill in humans a disposition to believe in him.

Many people fail to recognize this because of a confusion about the role chance plays in Darwinian evolution. Evolutionary theory asserts that some genetic variations are beneficial while most are not. Those organisms that receive the beneficial variations are more likely to survive and reproduce, thus passing on the beneficial genetic modifications to their offspring. The occurrence of the genetic mutations is random. So, one might think, if evolution requires a random process, then it cannot be controlled by anyone, even God.

This conclusion does not follow. When evolutionary theory asserts that the occurrence of genetic mutations is random, what is meant is that the mutations do not occur in response to the needs of the organism. A beneficial mutation does not occur because it is beneficial; indeed, the great majority of mutations are not beneficial. But to say that mutations are random in *this* sense is not to say that they are uncaused.[2] To the contrary, mutations occur on the basis of physical laws. But if God exists, God is the author of those physical laws as well as the matter those laws describe. Being omniscient, God must know what results will follow from the laws of nature he has instituted and the material stuff he has created, and thus nothing in the natural world is truly outside of God's control.[3] God is quite capable of designing a natural world in which his purposes are

2. For a clear discussion of this point, see Plantinga, *Where the Conflict Really Lies*, 11–12.

3. God may choose to extend free will to some of his creatures and thus decide not to determine their choices, but even in this case God is in control and could at any moment exercise control over any situation, even if this required him to limit human freedom.

fulfilled through natural processes. It is possible, then, to accept evolutionary theory and at the same time believe that God is the creator of the heavens and the earth.

In fact, not only is it true that evolution and creation are consistent, but evidence from evolutionary psychology suggests that humans have natural tendencies to form a belief in God or gods. Evolutionary theory thus gives at least some empirical confirmation of Calvin's idea of the *sensus divinitatis*. In the past, social scientists attempting to explain belief in God often tried to appeal either to psychological needs, as is the case for Freud, or to sociological functions, as can be seen in Durkheim. However, psychologists and cognitive scientists are increasingly arguing that a tendency to form religious beliefs has been hardwired into humans by the evolutionary process that has made us what we are.[4] We naturally respond to certain features of our natural environment by forming a belief in divine agents. Even children, to use the striking image of a contemporary psychologist, are "intuitive theists" prone to "promiscuous teleology."[5]

To be sure, the majority of scientists who are pursuing this research program are atheists who believe that these hardwired dispositions to form beliefs in God or gods are "spandrels," unintentional by-products of other features of our cognitive makeup that had evolutionary survival value. However, if God exists and has created us through an evolutionary process, there is no need to interpret these dispositions as useless; they could be the means whereby God gave us an ability to recognize his reality, and some researchers have recognized this possibility.[6]

---

4. For just one example out of a host of recent books, see Pascal Boyer, *The Naturalness of Religious Ideas: A Cognitive Theory of Religion* (Berkeley: University of California Press, 1994).

5. Deborah Kelemen, "Are Children 'Intuitive Theists'? Reasoning about Purpose and Design in Nature," *Psychological Science* 15 (2004): 295–96.

6. See Justin Barrett, *Why Would Anyone Believe in God?*, Cognitive Science of Religion (Walnut Creek, CA: Altamira, 2004).

One might object at this point that these natural tendencies to believe in God do not lead to belief in the true God but lead more often than not to what used to be called paganism and is now more apt to be called primal or tribal religion. After all, belief in God or gods may be pervasive among human cultures, but from a Christian point of view, true knowledge of God is not. To this objection I have two replies. First, Christian missiologists are increasingly inclined to see more value in primal religions than was previously the case. In many cases the believers in these faiths, when presented with the Christian gospel, see their former faith as preparation for the good news they have come to believe. They already believed in supernatural beings and even in a high or supreme God. What they did not know was that this God had revealed himself through his Son, Jesus of Nazareth.

The second response is this: perhaps the intended outcome of these natural signs is not a full, accurate knowledge of God at all but what I earlier called anti-naturalism. To understand God in the way we must in order to have a relation to him, our knowledge of him must be based on his self-revelation, not on the natural signs. The natural signs, then, are not intended to give us an adequate knowledge of God. They are intended only to give us a sense that there is more to reality than the physical world. They point us beyond the world to a mystery, but they themselves do not dispel that mystery. They are signs that prepare us to encounter God's self-revelation.

In chapter 2 I briefly described the contemporary philosophers of religion known as Reformed epistemologists, such as Alvin Plantinga. We are now in a position to give an interpretation of their claim that belief in God can be properly basic and not based on arguments or inference. The Reformed epistemologists see themselves as developing the claim of John Calvin that God has implanted in humans a *sensus divinitatis*, a natural tendency to believe in God. Perhaps this *sensus divinitatis* works through the natural signs that God has implanted in us. If this is right, then we can understand why the Reformed epistemologists insist that belief in God can be basic and not based on other beliefs.

Do Theistic Natural Signs Provide Evidence for God?

The fact that belief in God can be epistemologically basic does not mean that those beliefs have no ground at all. The ground of the beliefs is simply the natural signs that give rise to the beliefs. Does that mean these natural signs should be considered evidence for God? I believe the answer to this question should be yes, in two different senses. Recall the distinction made between propositional evidence and nonpropositional evidence in chapter 2. Let us first consider the question of whether the signs can provide propositional evidence. It is true that the signs can operate, as Reformed epistemologists affirm, to produce belief in a psychologically direct way, and when they do function in that way they are basic beliefs and do not rest on any propositional evidence. However, even though belief in God can be basic in this way, that may not be the case for everyone. For some people, for a variety of reasons, the signs may not be sufficient to produce belief in a direct and spontaneous way. However, it might be possible for some of those people to make the signs themselves the primary objects of their reflection. As they become aware of the signs, they can develop beliefs about the signs, and some of those beliefs might function as propositional evidence for God's reality. What happens in this case is that the signs are developed into arguments for God's existence. I believe that many of the arguments given for God's existence are in fact rooted in natural signs and gain their plausibility from the signs that the arguments are trying to articulate. When this happens the signs become the source of propositional evidence.

However, even in the case where the signs operate to produce belief in a more spontaneous manner, there is a sense in which they can be considered as evidence. Recall that when Reformed epistemologists say that belief in God need not be based on evidence, they are using the term "evidence" in the sense of propositional evidence, premises that can serve as the basis for an argument or an inference. In chapter 2 I claimed that there is also nonpropositional evidence consisting of experiences or even of physical objects, as when the police view fingerprints left at the scene of a crime as evidence. In this nonpropositional sense, even when not being employed as the basis for an argument, the natural signs for God's existence can be considered evidence, at least evidence for anti-naturalism.

So the natural signs for God can provide both propositional and nonpropositional evidence, even if it is true that they can give rise to beliefs in God that are properly basic. In the next chapter I will go on to describe some of these natural theistic signs and say something about their appeal.

4

Natural Signs for God and Theistic Arguments

In the last chapter I explained what a theistic natural sign is and suggested that such signs could be the means whereby the *sensus divinitatis* operates to produce belief in God. Although belief produced in this way can be properly basic, the signs can still be regarded as evidence for God in a nonpropositional sense. And if a person reflects on the signs, they might possibly be converted into propositional evidence.

It is now time to describe these theistic natural signs in some detail. What are the theistic natural signs, and how can we recognize them? I shall discuss five of them: the experience of cosmic wonder; the experience of purposive order; the sense of being morally accountable; the sense of human dignity and worth; and what I call the longing for transcendent joy. In this brief book I cannot do full justice to all five, though I have given a fuller account of some of them in other places.[1]

1. For a readable account addressed to a general audience, see my *Why Believe? Reason and Mystery as Pointers to God* (Grand Rapids: Eerdmans, 1996). For a more rigorous and well-developed account, see my *Natural Signs and Knowledge of God*.

If one wants to find signs for God's reality, one important place to look is the classical theistic arguments. I believe that natural signs for God can be seen as the source of the intuitions that give many of the arguments their force, and so if we look carefully at the arguments, we should be able to discern the signs that lie at their core. The arguments that have been given for God's existence are puzzling, in that they seem to have been refuted time and time again, and yet they continue to have appeal even to those who regard themselves as having refuted them. If natural signs lie at the core of these arguments, we can understand why this should be so. For the Easy Resistibility Principle implies that the signs will fail to provide coercive proofs; the person who is determined to avoid the conclusion can find a way to do so. Nevertheless, the signs lying at the core of the arguments continue to exercise their appeal and retain their force. If we find that even nonbelievers in many cases recognize the force of the signs, this will be an important piece of evidence that they do have genuine power.

Cosmic Wonder

The first sign I shall discuss is what I call the experience of cosmic wonder. There are times when it strikes almost everyone as strange and wonderful that the universe should exist at all. An experience of this sort might well start by reflecting on our own existence. It seems quite obvious that I might never have existed. My parents might have married other people or not gotten married at all. It is hard to imagine the world without me, but I know the world existed before I did and that it will most likely continue to exist after I have passed away. It seems that if things had gone just a bit differently, I would never have existed at all. Clearly I am what philosophers call a "contingent" being. I am the kind of being that exists but might never have existed.

However, when I think a little more deeply, I see that what is true of myself is true of everything else in the world. My parents, like me, might never have existed at all. Scientists say that if the evolutionary story had gone just a bit differently, humans would never have existed. Perhaps life of any kind might never have existed. If the initial configuration of the clumps of matter and energy coming out of the "Big Bang" that began the universe had been distributed a bit differently, perhaps there would have been no planet Earth, no solar system, no Milky Way galaxy. But why should there have been a Big Bang anyway? Why should anything at all exist?

This kind of thinking and the experiences that engender it lie at the core of traditional cosmological arguments, which take as their starting point our sheer wonder and amazement that there should be a universe at all. If theism is true, then the universe might never have existed; it is the result of God's free creative activity. Our sense of wonder when we experience the world is a true perception of the quality philosophers call "contingency" but that we might call the world's "might-never-have-beenness."[2]

Of course, the atheist is free to dismiss this experience and to claim that the world as such is just a brute fact. The world is contingent and cries out for an explanation, but there is no such explanation. They may recognize this sense of wonder but deny that it points to anything. However, even atheists such as Albert Camus are struck by the absurdity of this situation.[3] It appears even to them that the world ought to have a meaning, a reason for being, but their atheism leaves them only with the absurd. Camus tells us that "this world in itself is not reasonable; that is all that can be said. But what is absurd is the confrontation of this irrational and the wild longing for clarity whose call echoes

2. Evans, *Natural Signs and Knowledge of God*, 62.
3. See Albert Camus, "An Absurd Reasoning," in *The Myth of Sisyphus and Other Essays* (New York: Random House, 1955).

in the human heart."[4] It seems that, for Camus, we humans are constituted so that we feel the universe ought to have a certain character; that it does not have such a character seems absurd for him. Perhaps this "wild longing for clarity" that he speaks of is itself a natural sign, a clue that this universe is not intelligible by itself but points beyond itself to its maker.

Lest anyone think that such an experience is felt only by those strange thinkers we call "existentialists," I shall also cite the testimony of a distinguished contemporary analytic philosopher, J. J. C. Smart. Smart considers and rejects the cosmological argument for God's existence on the grounds that the argument requires the existence of a necessary being, a concept he says he can "make no sense of."[5] (However, I would add, his reasons for saying this are hardly decisive.) Nevertheless, although he rejects the *argument*, Smart acknowledges the force of the experience that drives the argument; he says that he "feels" the force of the question "Why is there anything at all?" even though he knows he cannot answer it.[6] His final position leaves him uneasy, wondering whether this experience is one that he should "cherish" or simply try to explain away.[7] His naturalism ought to lead him to the second option, but he clearly finds the experience in some way to be "deep" and does not wish to dismiss it. I believe he feels the force of a natural theistic sign.

Our sense of the mysteriousness of the sheer existence of the universe has precisely the characteristics one would expect to find in a natural sign. It is a widely available experience; almost everyone has it at some time. It naturally seems to point us beyond the universe to something or someone. But it is resistible.

---

4. Ibid., 21.
5. J. J. C. Smart, *Our Place in the Universe: A Metaphysical Discussion* (Oxford: Blackwell, 1989), 182.
6. Ibid., 183.
7. Ibid.

When we formulate the experience into an argument, those who wish to do so may reinterpret or dismiss the experience.

Purposive Order

The second natural sign I want to discuss is what I call the experience of purposive order, which lies at the core of the classical argument from design for God's existence. By this experience I mean the sense of wonder and mystery we sometimes gain when we look at the exquisite way a flower is organized or at the incredible intricacy of the human body and the way its different systems work together. A similar experience is commonly had when someone contemplates the beauty and grandeur of a majestic mountain range or gazes upon the awesome power of the ocean. These are surely experiences that virtually every human has had.

Such experiences naturally suggest that nature is the product of something that has some of the characteristics of a person. Intricate order that supports the achievement of some good seems purposive; it is simply apparent design. Apparent design suggests a designer. Biological organisms and their parts certainly do this. So also do magnificent mountain ranges and ocean vistas, which possess a beauty and sublimity that do not appear to be accidental. Such experiences naturally prompt humans to form a belief in God or gods.

Strikingly, this is true even for some people who reject the classical argument from design as a "proof" of God. David Hume and Immanuel Kant, who are often thought to be the people who refuted the classical argument from design, testify to the power of our experience of nature as purposive. Hume's fictional hero, Philo, in the *Dialogues concerning Natural Religion*, admits the power of this natural sign: "In many views of the universe and its parts, particularly the latter, the beauty and fitness of final causes strike us with such irresistible force that objections appear (what I believe they really are) mere cavils and sophisms; nor can we then imagine how it was ever possible for us to repose any weight on them."[8]

Kant offers similar testimony. In *Critique of Pure Reason*, in which he claims to have refuted the design argument as a conclusive proof, Kant nonetheless praises the argument in terms similar to Hume's: "Reason, constantly upheld by this ever-increasing evidence, which, though empirical, is yet so powerful, cannot be so depressed through doubts suggested by subtle and abstruse speculation, that it is not at once aroused from the indecision of all melancholy reflection, as if from a dream, by one glance at the wonders of nature and the majesty of the universe."[9] Both Kant's and Hume's are important testimonies, since they come from those one might call unfriendly witnesses. Hume very likely did not believe in God; he certainly was not a religious person by the standards of his day. Kant rejected any theoretical arguments for God's existence, though he did claim that a rational person who is committed to morality would believe in God as a "postulate." Nevertheless, both Hume and Kant recognize the force of the apparent design we see in nature. Genuine natural signs ought to have recognizable force, even though the evidence provided is resistible.

Does Evolution Undermine Design as a Natural Sign?

Of course our contemporary New Atheists may well respond by saying that Hume and Kant did not enjoy the benefits of our post-Darwinian perspective and so were easily deceived by

8. David Hume, *Dialogues concerning Natural Religion*, ed. Richard H. Popkin (Indianapolis: Hackett, 1980), 66.

9. Immanuel Kant, *Critique of Pure Reason*, trans. Norman Kemp Smith (New York: St. Martin's Press, 1965), 520 (A 624, B 652).

the appearance of purposive order in the universe. Evolutionary theory shows us, they might say, that the apparent design we see in nature is only apparent. However, it is not so clear that the theory of evolution disposes of our experience of the universe as purposive. Evolution, after all, is only an account of how the order we experience in the natural world came into being; it is not clear at all that this requires one to see this order as illusory. Why shouldn't we see natural selection simply as the process God has used to actualize the order that is actually present in nature?

Is the apparent purposeful order we see in nature an illusion? I shall argue that nothing in the scientific theory of evolution requires one to think that it is. The evolutionary process itself is one that depends on the laws of nature; the mechanisms that make the evolutionary process work depend, for example, on the existence of stable reproductive mechanisms, which in turn depend on the laws of physics and chemistry. Far from showing that the order in nature is illusory, evolution actually shows that the order we experience on the surface of things, so to speak, depends on a still deeper, hidden order.

The New Atheists, rather than taking the laws of nature for granted as a brute fact, ought to reflect more on the fact that the natural world seems "fine-tuned" to produce a world with beauty and value. Many of the laws of nature and the values of the constants that are part of those laws could have been very different than they are, yet they are precisely within the narrow range they must be in order to make possible living organisms and the complex systems that such organisms incorporate. This fine-tuning is itself a powerful argument for God's existence. It may not be a natural sign in my sense because the evidence is not widely available to those without a scientific education. Nevertheless, it at least suggests that it is a mistake to think that evolutionary theory defeats the claim that the natural world contains purposive order. If anything, it shows that the order we experience in nature is part of the deep structure of nature.

If our experience of the world as purposive is a natural sign for God, it does not depend on any argument or inference to function as it does, any more than our sensations of green grass require an argument to generate a reasonable belief in green grass. All that is required for the experience to function as a natural sign is that the order and purposiveness we perceive be actually present and that it be something that God has created so as to make it possible for us to become aware of his reality. All of this can surely be the case even if God has chosen to actualize that order through an evolutionary process.

The New Atheists, such as Dawkins, often seem to think that evolution and God are rival, mutually exclusive hypotheses about the origins of the natural world. Perhaps they think this because evolutionary theory posits that the process by which plants and animals have evolved requires random genetic mutations that are either selected or eliminated due to their survival advantages or lack thereof. Surely, they think, a process that depends on random mutations cannot be guided, and so God cannot have used an evolutionary means to achieve his ends.

However, as I have already argued, this argument fails. It depends on an equivocation in what is meant by "random." When scientists claim that genetic mutations are random, they do not mean that they are uncaused, or even that they are unpredictable from the point of view of biochemistry, but only that the mutations do not happen in response to the adaptational needs of the organism. It is entirely possible for a natural process to include randomness in that sense, even though the whole natural order is itself created and sustained by God. The sense of "randomness" required for evolutionary theory does not imply that the evolutionary process is outside of God's control.

Moral Signs

The rest of the natural signs I want to highlight lie within ourselves. In this section I will describe two that are connected to our moral lives and are linked to moral arguments for God. In my view these arguments are more powerful and convincing than contemporary philosophers are willing to admit.

Moral Obligation

One of these signs is simply our sense of moral obligation. It seems to us that we are morally obligated not to do certain things and obligated to do other things. I am morally obligated to honestly report my income to the income tax service. I am morally obligated not to spread false rumors about a rival for a job. Every decent person recognizes such obligations. It thus appears to us that we are responsible and accountable for our actions. It is natural to wonder: To whom are we responsible? To whom are we accountable? The obvious and natural answer is that we are responsible to God. I believe our sense of obligation is a natural sign that points to the one who has created us and has the authority to demand from us what is right and good.

Even atheists such as the late Australian philosopher J. L. Mackie acknowledge the force of these intuitions, which is why Mackie embraces an "error theory," in which he concludes that our ordinary moral beliefs are systematically mistaken.[10] Mackie does not see how objective moral obligations can come into existence as the product of a purely physical world, so he denies that there are any such things. Mackie acknowledges that our ordinary moral beliefs commit us to believing in such things, but he has the honesty and courage to declare that those beliefs are simply false.

10. See J. L. Mackie, *Ethics: Inventing Right and Wrong* (London: Penguin, 1977), esp. 31–42.

Of course, other contemporary secular moral philosophers have, with great ingenuity, developed moral philosophies that attempt to save the appearances of moral philosophy. In this brief book I cannot give a full account of these views and how they fail, but I will try to summarize some possibilities and sketch the problems they confront.[11] Some argue that morality is the product of evolution, claiming that creatures with moral instincts have survival advantages over those that do not. Such a view requires that evolution operates at the level of the group or the community rather than the individual, since it is obvious that moral behavior does not always favor the survival of the individual. However, such "group selection" is scientifically controversial. Even if this problem is solved, the evolutionary account explains only why humans *believe* they have moral obligations. Creatures with such beliefs are supposed to have survival advantages. But this is not an explanation of real moral obligations at all, since it is completely compatible with Mackie's error theory. Rather than explain objective moral obligations, the theory explains how we are duped by evolution to believe in such things.

An alternative evolutionary view stresses the idea that morality is reducible to altruistic behavior and claims that altruistic moral behavior is shaped by our genes. Since I share a lot of genes with my kin, and since evolution cares about the propagation of the genes, it is logical that I will behave in ways that help the members of my family or tribe. However, much of morality clearly extends beyond our family and tribe; most of us think we have at least some moral obligations to strangers, even people we have not met. Even if kin selection explained some of our tendencies to moral behavior, it could not explain why such behavior is sometimes obligatory.

11. For a fuller argument that secular accounts of morality fail, see my *God and Moral Obligation* (Oxford: Oxford University Press, 2013), 118–54. Also see my *Kierkegaard's Ethic of Love: Divine Commands and Moral Obligations* (Oxford: Oxford University Press, 2004), 223–98.

Other secular theorists try to explain morality in terms of a social agreement that is motivated by self-interest. Obviously, a society in which morality is widely flouted is not a nice community to be part of. Hence, it is often argued, it is in my own best interest to make an agreement to treat others in certain ways provided they agree to treat me well in return. There are many problems with such a view. First of all, one may ask when the agreement was made. Proponents of the view often respond that the agreement is not an actual, explicit agreement but one that people make implicitly in their interactions. However, it is unclear what content such a vague agreement would include. It is also hard to see why a person would be bound by such an agreement. There are certainly some occasions in which a person can do what is immoral without much fear that anyone will find out. The best strategy from a selfish point of view would seem to be to abide by morality when necessary but to selectively cheat on the agreement when one can do so without penalty. One cannot say that breaking the agreement would be immoral, since in this case the agreement is supposed to provide the foundation for morality.

The biggest problem with the social agreement view, however, is simply that many of my moral obligations are toward people who cannot benefit me in any way. I have moral obligations to the elderly and to those suffering from dementia, but such people cannot provide me any payback for my good behavior or penalize me if I fail to behave morally. In any case the agreement is an agreement to behave morally *if* others do the same. What if I am in a situation where other people are not behaving morally? It is well known, for example, that cheating is all too common in schools. If I am a student, should I tell myself that it is okay to cheat because others are cheating too?

There are, of course, other secular accounts of morality than these I have discussed, but in my judgment they are equally unsuccessful. For example, there is the "quasi-realism" of Simon Blackburn. Blackburn says that morality is a projection of human attitudes but that as a projection it has the appearance of an objective framework that can justify our ordinary moral language. However, a projection is still a projection, and it is hard to see how morality can acquire the objectivity and authority it appears to have on such a view.[12]

The unique character of moral obligations is generally recognized but hard to explain. Ronald Dworkin provides a clear example of what I mean by this. Dworkin distinguishes between happiness and what he calls "living well," a concept that he clearly understands as involving a moral dimension, and claims that we are *responsible* to do the latter: "We have a responsibility to live well and believe that living well means creating a life that is not simply pleasurable but good in that critical way."[13] The fact that we are responsible for living life a certain way looks like an obligation, but Dworkin seems baffled when he tries to account for this fact. It would be natural to think that the fact that we are responsible implies that we are responsible to someone, but Dworkin cannot fathom who that might be.

> You might ask, responsibility to whom? It is misleading to answer: responsibility to ourselves. People to whom responsibilities are owed can normally release those who are responsible, but we cannot release ourselves from our responsibility to live well. We must instead acknowledge an idea that I believe we almost all accept in the way we live but that is rarely explicitly formulated or acknowledged. We are charged to live well by the bare fact of our existence as self-conscious creatures with lives to lead.[14]

12. See my discussion of Blackburn in *God and Moral Obligation*, 123–29.
13. Ronald Dworkin, "What Is a Good Life?," *New York Review of Books* 58, no. 2 (February 10, 2011): 42. For a fuller discussion, see Dworkin, *Justice for Hedgehogs* (Cambridge, MA: Harvard University Press, 2011).
14. Dworkin, "What Is a Good Life?," 42.

Dworkin's reply seems only to deepen the mystery of moral obligation; what he offers seems more like elegant testimony to a perceived conviction that we are indeed subject to an obligation to live a moral life than an explanation of why we have such an obligation.

Suppose, however, that this sense that we are under moral obligation is a natural sign of God, an actual awareness of God's requirements for our lives. If that were the case, then we can understand why so many people through the millennia have thought that the moral life and the religious life were closely connected, such that the former depends on the latter. Dworkin clearly feels the force of this sign, which certainly seems to point to an authority to whom we are responsible, even if he refuses to follow the sign. If we make this sense of obligation a datum and try to explain it, we will have a moral argument for theism, and such arguments are powerful. In my view the sign is what underlies the argument and gives it that force, and the sign has power even for those who do not treat it as a datum to be explained but directly and spontaneously think of themselves as responsible and accountable to a moral authority.

Human Dignity

Another important theistic sign that is connected to our moral lives can be found in our sense that human beings as such have intrinsic worth and dignity, a view that underlies the claim that there are natural human rights. The intuition that humans possess this special moral status is widespread, even embodied in the United Nations' Universal Declaration of Human Rights. Interestingly, when the drafters of this statement were working on it, they were unable to come to any agreement about the basis of human rights and thus said nothing about it.[15] This

15. Nicholas Wolterstorff discusses this in his book *Journey toward Justice: Personal Encounters in the Global South* (Grand Rapids: Baker Academic, 2013), 130–34.

is understandable, since it is difficult for secular philosophers to explain why humans should have this special value. Kant famously attempted to ground human worth in reason, and many philosophers have followed him by claiming that what gives humans value are some capacities they have, such as reason. The problem with such a view is that humans who are incapable of reasoning or acting in productive ways, such as infants and older people suffering from dementia, nonetheless have a special worth and dignity that ground our obligations to treat them justly.

On the Christian view, humans are made in the image of God, who is both supremely good and the source of all other goods. If that is true, it is not surprising that humans have a deep worth and dignity that we can recognize, a value that mirrors the absolute value of God himself. Humans are literally signs of God, and the value and worth they have as God's image bearers points back to God himself.

Once again, I think this natural sign can function in two different ways. On the one hand, we can simply perceive humans as possessing a deep, profound value that points to their maker. We instinctively recognize that humans are not just meaningless clumps of matter; when a person dies, we feel that even the corpse should be treated with respect. If we reflect on this worth and try to explain it, we can again see this sign as generating a moral argument that has genuine force. The Christian view that humans are made in God's image makes sense of the fact that all humans, regardless of whether they are capable of reasoning, have a special worth.[16]

Søren Kierkegaard gives us a vivid image of the worth that humans have simply as humans in his book *Works of Love*.

16. For a powerful argument that an adequate view of justice can be grounded only in something like the Christian view that humans are made in the image of God, see Wolterstorff, *Justice: Rights and Wrongs*, 323–61.

Kierkegaard tries to express this idea that humans have a special worth in two ways: by speaking of an "inner glory" that all humans possess and by use of the image of a "common watermark."[17] He compares human life to a play.[18] In a play all the actors wear various costumes that befit their roles. One may play a beggar, while another plays a king. "But when the curtain falls on the stage, then the one who played the king and the one who played the beggar, etc., are all one and the same— actors."[19] Human life also contains a great "multifariousness," and some are indeed beggars, and others are kings. However, "when at death the curtain falls on the stage of actuality then they, too, are all one, they are human beings."[20] Each person, whatever their earthly differences, possesses an "inner glory." Every human being, according to Kierkegaard, can be compared to a fine piece of stationery:

> Take many sheets of paper, write something different on each one; then no one will be like another. But then again take each single sheet; do not let yourself be confused by the diverse inscriptions, hold it up to the light, and you see a common watermark on all of them. In the same way the neighbor is the common watermark, but you see it only by means of eternity's light when it shines through the dissimilarity.[21]

Perhaps Kierkegaard can be taken as suggesting that when we see our fellow humans as our "neighbors" in this way, we are sensing this "inner glory." The religious believer can clearly understand this perception of humans as possessing this "inner

---

17. The next few paragraphs are taken from my *Natural Signs and Knowledge of God*, 145–46.

18. Søren Kierkegaard, *Works of Love*, ed. and trans. Howard V. Hong and Edna H. Hong, Kierkegaard's Writings (Princeton: Princeton University Press, 1995), 86–89.

19. Ibid., 87.

20. Ibid.

21. Ibid., 89.

glory" because the believer sees humans as made in God's image. However, perhaps it is possible for someone who is not a believer, or who is not yet a believer, to perceive this basic human worth as well. Such a person can see the "light of eternity" that illuminates the "common watermark." In that case, perhaps the person is seeing the image of God, recognizing another person as made in God's image, even if the person does not realize that this is what he or she is seeing. In this way the person would be perceiving a natural sign for God: perceiving something that God created and intended to function as a pointer toward God, something that does indeed point toward God as the transcendent ground of the mysterious value we see in ourselves.

Joy

I shall describe only one more natural sign for God in this chapter: what C. S. Lewis calls "Joy." It is well known that Lewis, who had lost his childhood faith and became an atheist as a schoolboy, eventually came back to faith in God when he recognized that a particular experience he had savored all his life was really a longing for God. Even as a boy, Lewis, when reading certain poems or hearing music of a certain type, had experiences that were hard to describe. One of his first memories of this experience came from reading a line of poetry: "Balder the beautiful is dead, is dead."[22] Later he had the experience when reading Scandinavian mythology; it became linked to what Lewis calls "Northernness," a delight that is associated with the romance of this kind of myth, which he later experienced through some of Wagner's music.[23]

22. Lewis's search for Joy can be found in his autobiography *Surprised by Joy: The Shape of My Early Life* (London: Geoffrey Bles, 1955). The discussion of this line of poetry is on p. 23.
23. See ibid., 74–83.

The experience of Joy was a kind of longing for something that was always just out of reach, a transcendent reality that could not really be possessed. Lewis describes it as "an unsatisfied desire which is itself more desirable than any other satisfaction."[24] As a longing the experience was almost akin to something painful ("the stab, the pang, the inconsolable longing"), and yet Lewis found such happiness in the mere intimation of this mysterious something he called "Joy" that he wanted the experience more than anything in the world. Augustine famously said to God, "Thou hast made us for thyself and our hearts are restless until they rest in Thee."[25] Lewis understood his experience of Joy to be a sign that he and other humans are pilgrims; we are on a journey to another country that in this life we can only dimly grasp. He finally came to see Joy as an intimation of the God whom we are made to be united with and enjoy forever.

Lewis is hardly alone in this experience. Of course, many atheists appeal to this fact to criticize belief in God, seeing such belief as a form of wish fulfillment. The fact that we want to believe in God does not show that God is real, only that we have a need for a being like God. Lewis, however, was unfazed by this kind of attack. It is true, he admits, that a person's desire for something does not show that the person will get what he or she desires. A man on a life raft who is dying of thirst desperately desires fresh water, but he may not be able to find it unless he is rescued. However, it would be odd indeed if there were some natural desire, something basic to human nature, that could never be satisfied. The man on the life raft might not find water to drink, but it would be bizarre if he had a need for something that did not exist. Similarly, Lewis argues, a person might or

24. Ibid., 23–24.
25. Augustine, *Confessions*, 2nd ed., trans. F. J. Sheed, ed. Michael P. Foley (Indianapolis: Hackett, 2006), 3.

might not find God, but it would be very strange if people had a need for something that did not exist.[26]

It is instructive to compare Lewis's situation to that of the famous Spanish writer Miguel de Unamuno. Unamuno, like Lewis, had absorbed a kind of atheism as a student; he was influenced by a kind of scientific positivism that claimed that there was no rational basis for belief in God: "What enlightened person, nurtured by science, has faith?"[27] However, for Unamuno the intellect did not have the last word. Though he never fully recovered the firm faith of his childhood, he struggled to believe, and the ground of his struggle was his own need of God: "And if I believe in God, or at least believe I believe in him, it is because, more than anything else, I want God to exist, and because his existence is revealed to me in my heart."[28] Clearly, Unamuno recognized his own need for God as a kind of evidence for God's reality. Whether or not he fully believed, he felt the force of the sign.[29]

Conclusion

There are, I believe, other natural signs for God not commonly associated with arguments, such as our sense of gratitude for the goods of our lives and our sense of the beauty of the natural world. But perhaps I have said enough to show that, contrary to what the New Atheists say, there is evidence for God's existence, evidence that is precisely the sort we should expect to find. Even

26. C. S. Lewis, "The Weight of Glory," in *The Weight of Glory and Other Addresses* (New York: Macmillan, 1980), 32–33.

27. Miguel de Unamuno, "Diario intimo," in *Obras completas* [Complete Works], ed. M. Garcia Blanco (Madrid: Escelicer, 1966), 8:810.

28. Miguel de Unamuno, "Mi Religion," in *Obras completas* [Complete Works], ed. M. Garcia Blanco (Madrid: Escelicer, 1968), 3:261.

29. For a full account of Unamuno's struggle to believe, see Jan Evans, *Miguel de Unamuno's Quest for Faith: A Kierkegaardian Understanding of Unamuno's Struggle to Believe* (Eugene, OR: Pickwick, 2013).

if this evidence does not give us knowledge of the Christian God, it does suggest the reasonableness of anti-naturalism and the reasonableness of being open to a revelation from whatever reality there may be that these signs point to. In the next chapter I will turn to the question of how good the evidence for God is before turning in the final two chapters to questions about what a revelation from God might look like and how it could be recognized.

5

Can We Trust the Natural Signs for God?

In this chapter I will briefly address two questions: (1) Should we think of the natural signs as evidence for God, where "God" is a name for the mystery that transcends the natural order? (2) Assuming that the natural signs are evidence, are they good evidence?

The first question can be quickly dispatched. I have already argued that the signs can function as evidence in two different ways. They can become objects of critical reflection and generate arguments that take the signs as their basis. In this case the signs clearly furnish evidence in the sense of propositional evidence—premises from which God's existence can be reasonably inferred. However, the signs can also function in a more spontaneous and direct way. People can come to believe in God or gods on their basis without any kind of argument or inference. I think that this is in fact what Reformed epistemologists such as Alvin Plantinga have in mind when they claim that belief in God can be properly basic. On my interpretation, the natural signs are the means whereby Calvin's *sensus divinitatis* functions. I would argue that in this case also there is evidence for God's reality, only the evidence is nonpropositional in character. Such evidence provides rational support for a belief, but the belief is still psychologically basic and not the product of any conscious inference.

But what about the second question, which is by far the most important? Is the evidence provided by these natural signs good evidence, sufficient to ground reasonable belief? The answer one gives here will certainly be partly shaped by one's broader epistemology. The dominant epistemology of modern philosophy was classical foundationalism, exemplified in different ways by Descartes and Locke, the fathers of modern philosophy. Classical foundationalism seeks to provide an account of knowledge that shows how our most important beliefs can be derived from a foundation that is highly certain. The goal is to justify our knowledge claims by showing them as grounded in truths that any reasonable person should be able to know. This body of foundational truths is supposed to be knowable from an objective, disinterested standpoint and is supposed to provide a method for adjudicating all disputes about what counts as knowledge and what counts as justified belief.[1]

Let me say unequivocally that when measured by this standard, the natural signs for God do not provide either knowledge or justified belief. But the problem does not lie in the signs; it lies in the epistemology of classical foundationalism. Judged by the same standards, we do not have knowledge of the existence of an external world or that other people have minds. Of course, we do know that other people have minds and that there is an external world. But that knowledge is not based on

1. For a clear account and critique of classical foundationalism, see Alvin Plantinga, "Reason and Belief in God," in *Faith and Rationality: Reason and Belief in God*, ed. Alvin Plantinga and Nicholas Wolterstorff (Notre Dame, IN: University of Notre Dame Press, 1983), 16–93.

any arguments that start from premises that meet the standards of classical foundationalism.

There is no purely neutral perspective from which all the things we can know can be derived. I believe that these natural signs are evidence because they get us closer to the truth. They point toward God, and God is real. Some support for this is provided by the fact that many nonbelievers feel the "push" of the signs and recognize their power. However, I admit that the claim that the signs point us toward truth is made not from a neutral perspective but from the perspective of a believer.

Epistemology today is divided between "methodists" and "particularists." The methodists believe that before we can say we know anything about what we know, we must first give an account of knowledge and how knowledge is attained. We can then measure knowledge claims by this criterion and see which ones pass the test. We need a method that allows us to be sure we have genuine knowledge. The methodist wants some way to guarantee that our knowledge is genuine. Particularists, by contrast, claim that we first begin by knowing some particular things. Only afterward is it possible to reflect on our knowledge and develop an account of how we acquired it, just as in philosophy of art we begin by assuming that we know some art objects and then proceed to reflect on their nature and what makes them art. Obviously, particularists do not think it is possible to give a guarantee in advance that our knowledge is genuine.

I think the particularists are right. Their view entails having no absolute guarantees for our knowledge, and it seems to me that this accurately reflects the human condition. If we did not already know some things before we started doing epistemology, we could not possibly do epistemology. If we do not know anything until we have a theory of knowledge, we cannot achieve a theory of knowledge, because to know what knowledge is and how we get it, we must already know a lot. We must know something about truth, for example, and something about how humans can recognize truth when they find it.

What this means is that no a priori theory of evidence can tell us exactly when good evidence is good evidence. What makes evidence good evidence is that it tracks truth; when we follow the evidence we come closer to truth, or are likely to do so. But we only come to know that our grasp of truth is reliable through hard-won experience, and even this would be impossible unless we were committed to putting some trust in our human faculties. Good evidence is evidence that makes our beliefs more likely to be true, but until we have discovered some truths, we cannot know much about what makes a belief more likely to be true. Ultimately, our judgments about what counts as good evidence are linked to our judgments about what is true. The person who wants a guarantee that his or her beliefs are true prior to forming any beliefs is like a person who wants to know how to swim without ever getting in the water.

The other great divide in contemporary epistemology is the dispute between externalists and internalists. Externalists believe that what converts a true belief into knowledge is some fact about the relation between the knower and the external world. True beliefs that are the product of a reliable, truth-tracking process or the output of a properly functioning faculty aimed at truth are those that are warranted. Internalists believe that what justifies a belief is some fact that is internal to the knower's consciousness; to know, I must have evidence that is accessible to my consciousness.

I would argue that the natural signs for God can be good evidence from either perspective, whether a person is an externalist or an internalist. If there is a God who has created the signs and given us a natural disposition to respond to the signs with belief in God, then the externalist condition for warranted belief is satisfied. The signs are things that put us in touch with truth. Of course, that claim is not made from a neutral perspective, but there is no "view from nowhere" that is a purely disinterested view. If I am convinced that God is real, then the signs that produce belief in God are signs that track truth.

The situation with regard to things like sense perception and memory is actually very similar. I trust that what I believe through sense perception and memory is generally reliable. Why do I believe this? Because most of the beliefs I form by use of these faculties turn out to be reliable. But how do I know they are reliable? By using those faculties. There is an inescapable circularity in the human condition that implies that I must trust my faculties if I wish to avoid being a complete skeptic. That is how things look from an externalist perspective.

What about the internalist epistemological perspective? The signs work from this perspective as well, and here their value for someone who is not already a believer is more obvious. The signs are also things we have conscious access to. To many people, even including some nonbelievers, they seem to point to the reality of God. Here is one way of looking at the matter: when one perceives the signs, one has a disposition to see this world as one that God made. But that is just what evidence looks like from an internalist point of view. Evidence is simply what makes something evident.

A skeptic may object at this point that even if we have a natural tendency to view the world in a certain way, this does not logically imply that the world is that way. The signs could be natural illusions. The answer to this is that this is indeed possible. However, the signs are not supposed to provide proofs that would satisfy a classical foundationalist. They are resistible. The fact that it is *possible* that they are illusory is not a good reason to think they are.

Internalist epistemologies have been plagued by the threat of skepticism. Ever since Descartes, philosophers have wondered how we can know we are not living in a dreamworld or being deceived by an evil demon. How do we know we are not brains in a vat being stimulated by extraterrestrials, or that we are not living in the Matrix? The best answer to this skeptical threat requires the internalist to embrace what has been called the "principle of credulity," a principle that goes something like this: "All else being equal, it is reasonable to believe that reality is as it appears to us to be."[2] The natural signs are ways in which it appears to us that there is a God, and so, for some people at least, they provide evidence for God's reality. How powerful the evidence is will depend on how powerful the signs appear to be.

Here I can only offer personal testimony. For me, some of these signs are very powerful indeed. My sense of moral obligation, my experience of human persons as having intrinsic worth and dignity, my desire for eternal life—all these point me to my creator. However, it is significant that I am not the only one for whom the signs function in this way, and even more significant that some people acknowledge the force of the signs even though they are not believers.

Can the Evidence of the Signs Be Defeated?

The New Atheists often claim that one should not believe in God because such belief is simply a "blind leap of faith" that is not supported by evidence. I have responded to this by showing that there is evidence for God's existence. It is true that religious faith is a "leap" in the sense that it involves a commitment of the whole person; I will discuss this aspect of faith in later chapters. But it is wrong to say that faith is not supported by evidence, both nonpropositional and propositional.

2. For a good statement and defense of the principle of credulity, see Richard Swinburne, *The Existence of God*, 2nd ed. (Oxford: Oxford University Press, 2004), 303.

However, to say that one has evidence for a belief is not to say that one's overall evidence supports the belief. A man's fingerprints might be on a murder weapon, and this is evidence he is guilty of the crime. However, there might also be powerful evidence that the man was nowhere near the crime scene at the time of the murder, and thus the overall evidence may support the man's innocence. Similarly, an atheist might respond to my argument by claiming that even if we have some evidence for God's existence, our overall evidence makes unbelief more reasonable than belief.

It is true that a belief supported by evidence, even strong evidence, may be "defeated" by other evidence. It is natural then to wonder whether there are defeaters for belief in God. Accusations that this is the case are not hard to find.

Science and Religion

So what are the alleged defeaters for belief in God? One common claim is that belief in God is unscientific or is not compatible with a scientific worldview. However, it is difficult to find explanations of what the problem is and even more difficult to find convincing arguments for such claims. As we have already seen, to believe in God is to believe that the whole of the natural world, including both the whole of what exists and the orderly laws that govern what happens, is created by God and is continuously sustained by God. It is hard to see how any scientific finding could create a problem for belief in God in this sense. Science describes what exists and explains the behavior of the physical world by reference to laws of nature. It seems impossible in principle for science to discover that the things it investigates and the laws it discovers are not the result of God, since God is not an entity within the natural world that science investigates.

It is true, of course, that sometimes there have been conflicts between particular scientific theories and particular religious beliefs. Galileo's discovery that the solar system was not centered on the earth created problems with the church of his time. More recently, "creationists" who believe that God created the earth relatively recently have rejected evolutionary theory. However, it has not been difficult for religious believers to recognize that the alleged conflicts were the result of mistaken ideas about what religious belief really requires. No one today thinks that the earth revolving around the sun presents any kind of problem for belief in God, and there are many religious believers who see no problem in holding that God used an evolutionary process to create humans.

If there were some logical inconsistency between scientific findings and religious beliefs, it would be difficult to explain how it is possible that many of the greatest scientists, both in the past and today, have been religious believers. To give just two examples, physicist John Polkinghorne and biologist Francis Collins have published powerful works explaining why, as scientists, religious faith makes sense to them.[3] Alvin Plantinga has recently argued that there is no conflict between science and religious belief but that there are problems in combining a naturalistic worldview and science.[4] The naturalist has no good reason to trust that his or her faculties, if they are the product of evolution, are reliably aimed at truth. Unguided evolution cares only about survival; truth is not necessarily what helps us survive. The theist, on the contrary, has good reason to hold that our faculties, which are ultimately the work of God, whether created directly or through an evolutionary process, are reliable.

3. See Polkinghorne, *Belief in God in an Age of Science*, and Collins, *Language of God*.

4. Plantinga, *Where the Conflict Really Lies*.

The Problem of Evil

The most commonly alleged defeater of belief in God is the problem of evil. This problem has been recognized from ancient times, both by religious believers and by unbelievers. Even in the Bible the book of Job poses tough questions as to why God permits suffering. The unbeliever often poses the problem as a challenge that goes something like this: God is supposed to be all-powerful, all-knowing, and completely good. A good being would eliminate all the evil that such a being can possibly eliminate. God, being all-powerful, could eliminate all evil. Therefore, if God exists, there would be no evil. However, there is plenty of evil of many kinds, such as moral evil, natural disasters, disease, and suffering.

Actually, I believe that the problem of evil does not really rise to the level of natural theology, if this is understood as providing a defense of anti-naturalism, as I argued in chapter 1. If we went solely on the basis of the natural signs for God, we could reasonably believe that there is a God or gods beyond the natural world, but we would likely not be sure what God is like. For all we know, God might not be powerful enough to defeat evil, or might not even be good enough to care to do so. Many of the primal religions found in various human cultures include beliefs in gods of this sort. To generate the problem of evil, we need to know that God is like the God of Christianity, and it is not clear that natural theology gives us what we would need to create the problem. Once we know that the God beyond the natural world is the Christian God, the problem of evil does arise. However, it is also possible, as we shall see, that Christianity gives us resources for dealing with the problem.

However, since my ultimate aim is to argue that belief in the Christian God is plausible, I want to go ahead and discuss the problem of evil seriously. The atheist can state the argument in hypothetical terms, claiming that *if* the Christian God exists, then there would be no evil. The atheist says that a good God could and would eliminate all evil, yet evil exists. This looks like a proof of God's nonexistence, and some philosophers have thought that it is.[5] However, taken as a proof, the argument is unsound, because a key premise is false. It is not true that a good being always eliminates all the evil it can. A mosquito bite on my foot is an unpleasant thing. I could eliminate it by cutting off my foot. However, it would certainly not be good to do that. Why is that the case? Because losing my foot would be a greater evil than the mosquito bite. A good being does not eliminate all the evil possible but rather eliminates evils where this is possible without creating a greater evil or losing a greater good.

It is clear that God, if God exists, allows evil. Traditionally, believers have held that God does so in order to bring about some greater good or prevent some greater evil. But is this plausible? We do know of cases where it seems plausible to hold that the occurrence of some evil leads to some good that outweighs the evil. For example, parents sometimes choose to allow their children, when they have reached a certain age and level of maturity, to make choices about how to spend their own time and money. The parents do not insist on choosing which friends the children may associate with and might allow them to spend their money on video games or clothes. It is obvious that such a parental policy sometimes leads to evil, because sometimes the children make bad, even disastrous, choices. Nevertheless, it is arguable that the parents are justified in allowing this because without giving children the chance to make meaningful choices, the children cannot develop into mature, morally responsible adults, and that is a good whose value outweighs the evil that achieving this goal requires.

---

5. The literature on the problem of evil is vast. For those new to the subject, a good place to start would be Michael Peterson, ed., *The Problem of Evil: Selected Readings* (Notre Dame, IN: University of Notre Dame Press, 1992).

In a similar way, theologians have sometimes argued that much of the evil that happens in the world is due to human beings making bad choices. God has given humans the power to make some choices that are free, and the possibility of misusing the power of free will is inherent in having free will. Why does God give humans free will? The answer is that he wants them to have the dignity of being his friends and coworkers. The love for God and others of free persons is much more valuable than the "love" of a robot who is programmed to behave in a certain way. The existence of free beings who can be friends and coworkers of God is sufficiently good for God to grant humans freedom, even though he cannot give them freedom without allowing them to misuse their freedom.

Theologians have also argued that the achievement of a great good such as having a loving character is even more valuable if it requires overcoming obstacles. The value of something like courage requires us to face dangers of various kinds, and it is through facing such dangers that courage is developed. Similarly, a person who overcomes self-centered ways to become a loving person who genuinely cares about others has achieved something of great value, and the value of such a character seems enhanced by the fact that it was achieved through struggle. It does seem possible, then, that evils sometimes make great goods possible.

However, the unbeliever might not find this satisfying. Perhaps, it will be conceded, it is possible that evils make possible great goods, and so it is possible that an all-good, all-powerful being might allow some evils. However, the unbeliever might argue that it is unlikely that all the evils in our world in fact lead to greater good. William Rowe has famously argued that there are many evils that do not appear to lead to any good whatsoever.[6] He gives as an example a deer that dies painfully

6. William Rowe, "The Evidential Argument from Evil: A Second Look," in *The Evidential Argument from Evil*, ed. Daniel Howard-Snyder (Bloomington: Indiana University Press, 1996), 262–85.

as a result of a forest fire. Rowe admits that it is possible that all the evils that occur in the world could make possible some greater good or prevent some greater evil, but he claims that this just seems highly improbable.

Some philosophers have responded to Rowe by suggesting that it is not implausible to think that the evils we see make goods possible. Forest fires, for example, often play a key role in natural ecology; without periodic fires, forests could not flourish. In any case, forest fires and other natural disasters occur because of the laws of nature. Is this good? A religious unbeliever might think that a world that generally abides by such natural laws is less good than a world where natural objects could constantly change their properties. Such a person might ask, "Wouldn't it be good if water had one set of properties when we want to drink it but a different set of properties when a person was drowning and needed to breathe water?"

I would reply to the unbeliever that it is far from obvious that a world without natural laws would be a better world than ours. A world without natural laws would be a world in which objects do not have fixed, stable properties. However, a world in which natural objects had no fixed properties would be like a dreamworld. It would be a crazy, unpredictable world in which meaningful choice would be difficult or impossible, since one can make a meaningful choice only if the outcomes of one's choices are predictable.

The unbeliever might respond to this by claiming that natural laws are indeed good but that God could and should have given us a better set of laws. Perhaps with a different set of natural laws we would have fewer fires, hurricanes, tornadoes, and earthquakes. Perhaps this is true. But how do we know? Do we finite humans really know much about universe making? In the book of Job, God confronts Job and asks him some hard questions: "Where were you when I laid the earth's foundations?

Tell me, if you understand" (Job 38:4). The laws of nature form an interconnected whole; it is not clear that one can change one thing without changing everything. It seems rash to claim that we *know* that the evil in the world could be eliminated without losing greater goods or creating greater evils. How much do we humans really know about universe making?

It is true that many things happen in the world that make even believers in God wonder what God is up to. I am willing to concede that I cannot provide a clear and convincing "theodicy," an explanation of just how the evils that occur always lead to greater good or prevent greater evils. But what follows from the fact that I cannot provide a theodicy? Does it follow that God does not exist, or that it is unlikely that God exists? This would be the case only if the following principle were true: "If God had good reasons for allowing evil, I would know what they are." However, this principle seems far from obviously true or even probable. It is a commonplace that a young child is often unable to understand the actions of an adult, even if the adult is wise and has only the child's good in mind. The adult may have the child vaccinated in order to prevent the child from getting a potentially fatal disease, but the child may not understand this, since the child does not have a clear grasp of concepts such as disease and death. The child knows only that the needle hurts!

However, the difference between a human child and a human adult is a relative one, in that both have finite intellects. The difference between a human mind and God's mind is vastly greater, for God's mind is infinite according to the Christian view of God. It is by no means surprising that we humans do not fully understand God's goals for us and the universe or his means for achieving those goals. One huge difference between God and humans is, of course, that we are temporal and mortal beings, while God is eternal. There is no reason to think that

God's purposes for humans are exhausted by their time on earth during this life. Christianity has always taught (and here we must remember that the problem of evil is generated by accepting that God is like the God of Christianity) that God has destined humans for eternal life, and it certainly seems possible that, if earthly life is preparation for an eternal life of happiness, many of the evils of this life could be outweighed in eternity in ways that we cannot currently grasp.

Of course, if we do not have a convincing theodicy, our belief that this is so requires a degree of faith or trust in God's goodness. Whether such faith is reasonable will depend on what we know about God and God's character. I believe I know my wife and her character well. I know she is good and she loves me. If she performed some act that seemed unloving that I could not explain, I might still be reasonable to trust her because of my knowledge of her.

In a similar way, if God acts in ways we do not understand, it may still be reasonable to trust God, especially if we have gotten to know something about God and God's character. I said at the beginning of this section that it is a belief in the Christian God (or a God like the Christian God) that generates the problem of evil. However, if Christianity is true, we do have knowledge of what God is like because God has revealed something about himself to us humans. He has in fact become a human and suffered a cruel and painful death, all on our behalf, motivated by sheer love for us. God has given us reason to believe he is a God who is good and loving.

According to Christianity, this is not something God has communicated to us merely in words. It is something he has shown by his actions. Suppose that I am trapped in some painful circumstances. A friend writes me a letter assuring me that he cares about my suffering and is thinking about me. That would be good, of course. But it would be far better if my friend showed me his concern and love by coming to be with me and suffering with me. Christianity says that this is exactly what God has done in Jesus. God not only tells us that he is loving and that our sufferings have a point; he also shows us this is true by sharing in our sufferings.

Of course, the skeptic may point out, rightly, that this is all true only if Christianity is true, and that requires the Christian revelation to be true. This raises the all-important question of how one might come to know what God is like. I have argued that it is reasonable to accept anti-naturalism and to believe that there is something or someone beyond nature on the basis of the natural signs for God. However, I have agreed that if we had to rely solely on these natural theistic signs, our knowledge of God or the gods would be uncertain and unreliable.

If there is a God, and God wanted us to know him, he would want to remedy this situation by giving us knowledge of himself that is clear and reliable. We need to know what God is really like and how we should develop a relationship with him. Christianity says that this is exactly what God has done. God has taken the initiative by revealing himself to us.

Of course, there are many religions in the world, and many of them claim to have a true revelation from God. How can we know that an alleged revelation is genuine? That is the question to which I shall turn in the next chapter.

6

Recognizing God's Self-Revelation

In chapter 2 I argued that Christians should welcome natural theology so long as the goals of natural theology are modest. Natural theology should primarily be conceived as providing support for anti-naturalism, shaking up the dogmatic confidence of the New Atheists that naturalism and materialism are the default rational views of the universe. I also argued that if God exists, we would expect to have evidence for God's reality that would satisfy two "Pascalian constraints." The evidence would be widely accessible but also easily resistible.

In chapter 3 I argued that there are natural signs that point to God's reality and that such signs do satisfy these Pascalian principles. They are widely present in human experience and easy to recognize. However, they can also be ignored, discounted, or misinterpreted. They do not point clearly and unambiguously to God for all people, and even when working properly they do not necessarily lead to reliable knowledge of God and his character. In many cases they may produce a belief in gods of all kinds. But the signs do point beyond the natural world to a mystery that lies behind that world.

In chapter 4 I argued that these natural signs provide evidence for God's reality, at least for a belief in some kind of God or gods. Our experiences of cosmic wonder and of purposive order, our sense of moral accountability and of human dignity and worth, and our desire for eternal life all point to God's reality. I believe that when these signs are properly interpreted, they point with force to a personal God who is beyond the universe. This conclusion is consistent with the biblical revelation itself. Romans 1:20 affirms that God's reality can be "clearly seen" from what God has made, and in Psalm 19 we are told that the "heavens declare the glory of God" and that they "pour forth speech" that can be heard all over the earth.

However, even if these signs are such that it should be possible for anyone to know God's reality, it is obvious that not everyone does know God. There are plenty of atheists around, and human history is replete with those who knew that there was a God or gods but had very mistaken ideas about God's character. Even when they are functioning as they should, the theistic natural signs do not give us the kind of knowledge of God that makes it possible to have a personal relationship with God. Their function should be to open our hearts and minds to the mystery that lies behind the natural order; we should long to know more about the "unknown god" Paul speaks about in Acts 17.

Christians have traditionally held that the knowledge of God we humans need is made possible through God's self-revelation, a revelation given in history through the calling of Abraham and the formation of his descendants as a special people of God; through Moses and the prophets; and decisively in Jesus of Nazareth and the community founded by his chosen followers, the apostles. They have also affirmed that God's revelation comes to us in verbal form as well in the Old and New Testaments, inspired by God as a trustworthy witness to salvation history and a guide for those who want to serve God. Although it is quite important that God's revelation occurs in history and not just in a book, in what follows I am going to focus largely on the Bible as the locus of God's self-revelation for Christians. Certainly God has revealed himself in history and not just in writing, but without the written record our knowledge of that historical revelation would be scanty.

Interpreting the Bible

Before going on to consider how one might recognize a special revelation such as the Bible as truly coming from God, I first make some qualifications as to the role a special revelation plays in coming to know the truths of Christian faith. It is clear, I think, that unless God had done something to reveal himself to us more clearly, we would not have much in the way of reliable knowledge of God. Christians believe that this self-revelation comes mainly through the Bible, and thus it makes sense to focus my attention on why one should believe the Bible is such a revelation. However, I do not want to suggest that merely having the Bible, even if it is an authentic revelation from God, would automatically and immediately make it possible to know all the important doctrines that Christians proclaim. Christians proclaim that God is a Trinity: three persons in one substance. They proclaim that Jesus of Nazareth is God incarnate, one person with both a divine and a human nature. And, of course, there are many other important Christian doctrines, such as the claims that God will raise humans bodily from the dead and that Christ's death and resurrection atone for human sin.

It is generally not possible for Christians to come to know such things without the Bible, or at least without some other reliable testimony that traces back to the apostles, the earliest followers of Christ whom Christ himself selected to carry on his work. However, it is not enough just to *have* the Bible. To gain such knowledge the Bible must be read and understood; this means it must be properly interpreted. An unbeliever might at this point argue that this is a very difficult task and that this is shown by the great variety of ways the Bible has been interpreted, including all those readings the church has judged to be wrong and even heretical. So the question of how to interpret the Bible must be faced. Even if we knew the Bible to be an authentic revelation from God, this question would still have to be faced.

A number of answers to this question have been given. One important answer is that although the Bible is certainly a long and complex book and has many obscure passages, the main thrust of God's message is nevertheless clear enough to an individual who is seeking God. This is what Protestant Christians mean when they argue for what is called the "perspicuity of Scripture." The idea is not that everything in the Bible is clear but that the most important things are clear enough for the honest seeker to grasp; such a seeker must believe in Jesus as one sent from God and try to follow Jesus. This claim about the clarity of Scripture is usually accompanied by a claim that the Spirit of the God who gave this revelation will also help guide the person who is seeking the truth.

It would be a mistake, however, to think of the Bible as a special revelation that God grants to isolated individuals who have to figure out what it means on their own. If God is going to give humans knowledge about himself through a revelation, it makes sense that he would also create a community to pass along that revelation and to help people understand it. That community is, of course, the church. The witness of the Spirit is normally exercised in and through the church, which is not to say that the Spirit cannot work in other ways. It would be pointless for God to grant a revelation without seeing to it that the revelation would be preserved and interpreted correctly. So the answer to the question as to how the Bible should be interpreted is this: it should be interpreted as the church has generally understood it.

It is important to recognize that the teachings Christians believe are contained in or derivable from the Scriptures were already being proclaimed by the church even before the Bible as a distinct book was recognized as authoritative. The teachings contained in the Bible had been passed down by the church from the apostles, and these teachings had already been summarized by the church in the early ecumenical creeds (such as the Nicene Creed), which were accepted by all the major branches of Christianity. Sometimes these early teachings of the church are described as "the rule of faith." So another way of answering the question of how the Bible should be interpreted is that it should be understood "in accordance with the rule of faith."[1]

When I say that the Bible should be interpreted as the church has interpreted it, it is of course fair to ask, "Who constitutes the church?" Some assert that the true church is the Roman Catholic Church or the Eastern Orthodox churches or various strands of Protestantism. My own view is that the true church consists of all those baptized disciples of Christ who are in communion with communities of faith that affirm the claims made by the early church in the ecumenical creeds. Whether or not I am right about what constitutes the true church, I believe that one can still say that the "rule of faith" that should govern biblical interpretation is given in those early ecumenical creeds. For even those Christians who disagree about what constitutes the true church can agree about this early "rule of faith" and its authority. This will, I think, give us something like "mere

1. For a more detailed argument for the claims made in this section, see C. Stephen Evans, "Canonicity, Apostolicity, and Biblical Authority: Some Kierkegaardian Reflections," in *Canon and Biblical Interpretation*, ed. Craig Bartholomew, Scott Hahn, Robin Parry, Christopher Seitz, and Al Wolters (Grand Rapids: Zondervan, 2006), 146–66.

Christianity" in the sense in which C. S. Lewis uses the term in his well-known book of that title.

Of course this does not mean that there will be no differences in how the Bible is interpreted. We all know that Christians have interpreted various passages differently and continue to do so. However, despite those differences it is possible to recognize a core of beliefs that all the churches that continue to affirm the ecumenical creeds have in common. All historic branches of Christianity affirm that God is the creator of all things other than himself, that God is three in one, that God has revealed himself through the history of Israel, and that God acted decisively in Jesus to redeem a lost humanity. They all believe that Christ was raised by God from the dead and that Christ will return to bring about God's final victory over evil. This is what the church believes God has taught us through the Bible.

Why should we accept the church's interpretation of the Bible? Not because we can scientifically or "objectively" prove that it is correct through some scholarly process but because the Bible is religiously important only if it is what it claims to be and what the church has claimed it to be. It makes no sense to hold that God would give us such a revelation and not provide a community to preserve it and interpret it. In some sense the Bible is the church's book, and it is this interpretation of the Bible that defines Christianity. If we want to know whether Christianity is true, it is this interpretation that we must consider.

The Problem of Multiple Revelation Claims

However, all of this assumes that the Bible is what Christians proclaim: a true special revelation from God. And that brings us back to our original problem, which is created by multiple claims by various religions to have a true revelation from God. As our increasingly shrinking world makes us all too aware, there are other claimants to the status of divine revelation: the Qur'an and the Book of Mormon,[2] for example, not to mention the sacred writings of India. Then there are alleged revelations like the one sitting in my office at home that was sent to me a few years ago by a would-be prophet, entitled *Salam: Divine Revelations from the Actual God.*[3] Even if we believe that the existence of a God or gods is reasonable, how could we recognize a revelation from God if God gave us one, particularly in view of the fact that there are multiple candidates for such a revelation?

Reformed epistemologists, led by Alvin Plantinga, have given an important answer to this question. Following Calvin, they have argued that a response to God's self-revelation is grounded not in evidence at all but in the internal testimony of God's Spirit, who produces a conviction of the truth of the gospel in the minds and hearts of Christians by giving to them the gift of faith. Just as belief in God can be properly basic and not the result of arguments or inferences, so belief in Christ can be properly basic, rooted in the witness of the Holy Spirit and not based on any kind of evidence or arguments for the truth of the Bible or the historicity of the events it describes. Plantinga goes on, in *Warranted Christian Belief*, to argue that beliefs produced in this way can be justified and can even amount to knowledge, since he defends an externalist account of knowledge as true belief produced by a properly functioning faculty—and one cannot imagine a more reliable faculty than one grounded in God's Spirit.[4]

I believe that Reformed epistemologists are, in an important way, profoundly right; genuine Christian faith is a gift of God

---

2. Of course, Mormons do not see this book as a rival revelation to the Bible but rather as an additional revelation.

3. Silvan D. Buxani, *Salam: Divine Revelations from the Actual God* (New York: SAU Salam Foundation, 2003). This book contains a lot of surprising information. For example, I would never have guessed that God was deeply opposed to the graduated income tax.

4. See Plantinga, *Warranted Christian Belief*, esp. 241–356.

and not a direct or immediate product of the consideration of evidence. However, to say that faith is a divine gift is not to say that one of the means whereby the Spirit of God produces faith might not involve or even require evidence. We can even go further and say that the testimony of the Spirit is itself a kind of evidence. I shall return to this issue later.

Right now I simply want to say that as a response to the New Atheism, the stance of Reformed epistemology at least *appears* to be rhetorically weak. The New Atheists ask for evidence; Reformed epistemologists say no evidence is necessary. Even if this answer is correct (and in an important sense I believe it is), it might give rise to the misleading impression that no evidence can be given. This does not follow logically, however. To say faith does not *need* to be based on evidence is not to say that it cannot be partly based on evidence or that evidence cannot play a valuable role in its development.

In any case, even firmly committed Christians sometimes find themselves struggling with doubts. One might wonder, for example, given that the Muslim or Hindu seems equally convinced of the truth of her faith, how one can be certain that what one believes is true. To be sure, one important way of dealing with doubt may be to ask God for reassurance in the form of a stronger awareness of the testimony of God's Spirit. Once again, however, it is important to remember that one of the ways God's Spirit might work in our lives is by helping us to see and understand the evidence that points to the truth of the gospel.

Even if my belief in the Bible as God's Word is primarily based on the testimony of the Spirit, it does not follow that doubt is impossible. Even Christians who believe that the Bible is God's Word may sometimes wonder if this conviction has really been produced by God or is simply a product of the ordinary factors that social psychologists say shape our beliefs, such as the groups we associate with or the people who raised and nurtured us. To be sure, God might use such ordinary means to produce faith, so to claim that a belief is influenced by peers or parents does not mean God is not involved. However, one way God might help a person resolve doubts would be to help that person see evidence that points to the truth.

A claim that a belief is based on the testimony of God's Spirit is certainly not immune to doubt. Such doubt is not necessarily a lack of faith that what God witnesses is true; it can, rather, be a doubt as to whether what I believe is really the result of God's witness. In the current intellectual world many scholars claim to have evidence that shows the Bible is untrustworthy, either morally or with respect to what it teaches about history or God.[5] Such claims are potentially what philosophers call "defeaters" for the claim that a belief is a result of God's Spirit. Even if a consideration of evidence is not the primary basis for a belief in the Bible as a revelation from God, it might be important in considering these alleged defeaters. Likewise, even if Reformed epistemologists are correct in asserting that no evidence is needed, there is still value in looking at the evidence that the Bible is a revelation from God, recognizing that the testimony of God's Spirit may itself be a kind of evidence.

However, before turning to a consideration of the evidence, I want to make one other important point. Christians do not think that it is important merely to believe the contents of what God has revealed. They think that *how* people come to believe what God has revealed is equally important. The process by which a person comes to believe what God has revealed is one in which a person learns to trust God and therefore develops a

5. See ibid., chap. 12, for a discussion of whether historical-critical biblical scholarship provides a defeater for the view that the Bible is known to be true through the testimony of the Holy Spirit. Also see Evans, *The Historical Christ and the Jesus of Faith* for a discussion of whether such scholarship undermines faith in the story of Jesus.

special kind of relationship with God. It is that relationship and not merely the believing that is important. I shall say something about why this is the case in the next section.

The Revelation-Authority Principle

In the *Summa Contra Gentiles* Thomas Aquinas distinguishes two kinds of truths about God.[6] Some truths "exceed all the ability of the human reason," while there are others that "the natural reason also is able to reach." Although in principle the second kind of truth could be grasped independently of divine revelation, Aquinas thinks it is good that God has revealed both kinds of truths. With respect to truths that reason could in principle know, God's revelation provides a way for all humans to know these truths in less time, with less admixture of error, and with greater certainty than would otherwise be possible.[7] However, truth that exceeds the power of human reason must be believed "only because God has revealed it."[8] There is no other way to acquire such truths.

Aquinas's view that there are revealed truths that should be believed because they have been revealed is a standard part of the Christian tradition. John Locke, for example, defines faith as "assent to any proposition, not thus made out by the deductions of reason, but upon the credit of the proposer, as coming from God in some extraordinary way of communication."[9] If we move to contemporary times, Richard Swinburne affirms that Christianity not only proposes a body of doctrine that "is to be believed on the grounds that it has been revealed" but is

---

6. Thomas Aquinas, *Summa Contra Gentiles*, trans. Anton C. Pegis (Notre Dame, IN: University of Notre Dame Press, 1991), I, 3, 2.

7. *Summa Contra Gentiles* I, 4, 1–5.

8. *Summa Contra Gentiles* I, 9, 2.

9. John Locke, *An Essay concerning Human Understanding* (Kitchener, ON: Batoche Books, 2001), 576. The passage is in book 4, chap. 28, sect. 2.

in fact the only major religion whose primary tenets are supported in this way.[10]

I refer to the claim that the contents of a divine revelation should be believed because they have been revealed as the "Revelation-Authority Principle." The Revelation-Authority Principle has two valuable implications. First, it gives a plausible account of how humans might rationally come to believe truths that they could never discover through the exercise of their own unaided faculties. A revelation known in this way could thus remedy the defects present in our natural awareness of God. Second, it connects belief in the content of a revelation with trust in God and thus contributes to an understanding of how faith could be a virtue. It seems mysterious that mere propositional belief could be virtuous, but less mysterious if such belief is made possible by trust.

Undermining the Revelation-Authority Principle

It seems possible to give arguments for the authenticity of a purported revelation that in fact undermine the Revelation-Authority Principle. Suppose, for example, that someone gave the following argument in support of some revelation R: "One would expect a genuine revelation from God to contain all truths and no falsehoods. All the contents of R can be demonstrated by reason to be true independently of their presence in R. So R is a genuine revelation from God." The problem with this argument is not merely that as a deductive argument it is invalid but also that if it were successful (perhaps reconstrued as an inductive or probabilistic argument), it would no longer be necessary, and maybe not even possible, for the person who knows about the demonstrations to believe the contents of R *because* they have

10. See Richard Swinburne, *Revelation: From Metaphor to Analogy* (Oxford: Oxford University Press, 1992), 95.

been revealed. At least it will not be possible to believe by faith something that is known to be true by proof.[11] If everything in R (or everything religiously important) can be known independently of R, then R has no essential importance.

To be sure, the fact that *parts* of a revelation could be confirmed independently of the revelation would not necessarily undermine the Revelation-Authority Principle. So, if a revelation contains some things that can be known by reason, as Aquinas maintains, then the fact that those parts of the revelation can be "checked out," so to speak, might be part of an argument for the authenticity of the revelation. Richard Swinburne does in fact say that this is one way that the Christian revelation could be defended as genuine.[12]

However, as Swinburne admits, the evidence for a revelation provided in this way would be weak.[13] The fact that a prophet says *some* things that can be independently ascertained to be true does not go far toward showing that *everything* the prophet says is true, since "teachers who teach deep truths teach falsities also."[14] The fact that a text contains some true content provides even less in the way of evidence for a claim that this text is inspired by God and has special authority. Furthermore, it would seem that the greater the portion of a revelation that can be confirmed independently, the less significant the revelation would be, for as Swinburne tells us, a "revelation seeks to tell us deep things that we cannot find out for ourselves—and it would be a fairly thin revelation if its only role was to suggest things that we could immediately check."[15]

---

11. This assumes that what is known on the basis of a proof cannot simultaneously be believed on the basis of authority. Thomas Aquinas endorses this claim in *Summa Theologica* II-II, 1, 4–5.

12. Swinburne, *Revelation*, 86.

13. Ibid., 89.

14. Ibid.

15. Ibid., 88.

Aquinas says that a true revelation from God will contain things that "surpass human reason" because "we only know God truly when we believe him to be above everything that it is possible for man to think about him."[16] So according to Aquinas, a revelation from God that consisted solely, or perhaps even substantially, of truths that could be learned apart from revelation would not only undermine the Revelation-Authority Principle but also give us a misleading picture of God. All of this suggests something like a dilemma. If a revelation contains a small amount of independently verifiable content, this provides only weak support for the authenticity of the revelation. To provide impressive support, the amount of such content would have to be a predominant part of the revelation. However, to the degree that the amount of such content increases, the value of the revelation decreases.

The worry that certain "defenses" of a revelation might actually undermine the revelation by undermining the revelation-authority principle is no idle one. One can plausibly argue that some of the claims made in the eighteenth and nineteenth centuries in support of religious belief generally, and even those allegedly made on behalf of Christianity in particular, had just this effect. Immanuel Kant, for example, in *Religion within the Limits of Reason Alone*, set himself the task of seeing what religious truths, perhaps originally believed because they had been revealed, could be affirmed on the basis of reason independently of any historical revelation. Whatever Kant's own intentions may have been, if someone thinks this experiment provides results that are religiously adequate, then that person would be freed from the necessity of believing anything because it has been revealed.

A second example may be found in the theological method of Friedrich Schleiermacher. Schleiermacher, at least on many

16. *Summa Contra Gentiles* I, 5, 3.

interpretations, attempted to look at the Christian revelation as the outcome of religious experiences of a certain kind, experiences that are in principle generally available. Those who replicate those experiences can believe the contents of the Christian revelation on the basis of those experiences, and thus it is no longer necessary to believe those contents because of the authority of the authors of the revelation.

A third example is provided by G. W. F. Hegel, or at least as Hegel was understood by Kierkegaard. Hegel attempted to vindicate the Christian religion, but he did so by trying to show that the truths contained in the Christian revelation are essentially identical to the insights one can arrive at through his own speculative, dialectical philosophy. To Kierkegaard the implication was that the unreflective faith of ordinary Christians was supposed to be vindicated by Hegel's speculative reinterpretation of that faith. On such a view, ordinary believers may still find it necessary to believe what has been revealed because it has been revealed, but speculative philosophers can "go beyond" this kind of faith.

According to Kierkegaard, this undermining of the revelation-authority principle is not only to be found in the writings of philosophers and theologians but also has somehow seeped into the sermons of the parish priests:

> From the scholarship the confusion has in turn sneaked in to the religious address, so that one not infrequently hears pastors who in all scholarly naiveté . . . prostitute Christianity. They speak in lofty tones about the Apostle Paul's brilliance, profundity, about his beautiful metaphors etc.—sheer esthetics. If Paul is to be regarded as a genius, then it looks bad for him; only pastoral ignorance can hit upon the idea of praising him esthetically, because pastoral ignorance has no criterion but thinks like this: If only one says something good about Paul, then it is all right.[17]

17. Søren Kierkegaard, *Without Authority*, trans. and ed. Howard V. Hong and Edna H. Hong (Princeton: Princeton University Press, 1997), 93. This quotation is from

Kierkegaard agreed with Aquinas and the standard Christian view that Paul should be believed because Paul is an apostle and, as such, has authority. On Kierkegaard's usage, a "prophet" is someone authorized by God to speak on behalf of God, and an "apostle" is someone who has been given this prophetic authority directly by Christ. To appeal to Paul's eloquence or logical brilliance as a basis for believing him is to confuse an apostle with a genius, two categories that are qualitatively different. Kierkegaard made the point clearly and wittily: "As a genius, Paul cannot stand comparison with either Plato or Shakespeare; as an author of beautiful metaphors, he ranks rather low; as a stylist he is a totally unknown name—and as a tapestry maker, well, I must say that I do not know how high he ranks in this regard."[18]

One might think—and even hope—that such confusions were typical of the nineteenth century and that they have now been put behind us. Alas, I fear that this is not the case. Sermons in which the Bible is recommended on the grounds that it provides excellent commonsense advice for life are all too common in my experience, at least in conservative, pietistic Protestant churches. And one gets the impression that in certain liberal theological circles, the idea of forming a belief solely because the content of the belief has been revealed by God would not even receive a hearing. Even theologians whom most would regard as moderate seem too easily to undermine the Revelation-Authority Principle. I shall give two examples, but it would not be difficult to come up with many others.

In Lee McDonald's *The Formation of the Christian Biblical Canon*, a book that has been widely used as a text in seminaries

---

an essay entitled "The Difference between a Genius and an Apostle" that Kierkegaard published as part of *Two Ethical-Religious Essays*, and it is a revision of a section of *The Book on Adler*.

18. Kierkegaard, *Without Authority*, 94.

and religion departments, the author poses the question of whether we should consider adding to the biblical canon by including such books as the *Gospel of Peter* and the *Gospel of Thomas*.[19] I assume here that a decision about what belongs in the canon is a decision about what possesses divine authority. McDonald seems at least mildly suspicious of proposals to expand the canon, but what is noteworthy in the present context is that the basis on which he thinks the decision should be made seems to be one that undermines the Revelation-Authority Principle:

> For some of us, however, the matter has to do with whether what is offered as a candidate for future inclusion could in fact improve our current picture of Jesus. Would, for example, the inclusion of the *Gospel of Peter* or the *Gospel of Thomas* in our biblical canon be an advantage or disadvantage? Do they significantly add to our understanding of who Jesus was, what he did, and what he asked from his followers?[20]

McDonald seems to say that whether a book should be added to the canon, and thus be regarded as having authority, should be determined by whether it gives us new, reliable historical information, and it appears that he thinks this question is one to be determined by historical scholarship. But in such a case one would believe the contents of, say, the *Gospel of Thomas* not on the basis of God having authorized the book but on the basis of contemporary historical scholars having judged the book as historically reliable.[21]

19. See Lee Martin McDonald, *The Formation of the Christian Biblical Canon* (Peabody, MA: Hendrickson, 1995), xviii.

20. Ibid.

21. McDonald actually seems to imply an additional criterion for canonical authority when he suggests that *Thomas* would probably get a negative vote because its ending is offensive to women readers today (see *Formation*, xviii). The practice of rejecting—or accepting—the contents of a book because readers find those contents to be either to their liking or offensive is clearly different from a practice of accepting those contents because they have been revealed by God.

My second example comes from normative theology. Timothy Jackson, in his well-regarded book *The Priority of Love: Christian Charity and Social Justice*, often cites New Testament passages that support his major thesis, aptly summarized in the title. However, Jackson does not hesitate to reject Paul's argument (in 1 Cor. 15:12–14) that the Christian life rests on the hope of resurrection.[22] Why does he reject Paul on this point? Apparently he does so on the basis of an ethical principle that he holds and that Paul evidently did not—namely, that one must not "instrumentalize the virtue of love" and that it would be a "betrayal of charity to hold that it [charity] must eventuate in a postmortem afterlife."[23] To me it appears that Paul's authority here is subordinated to that of a philosophical principle, a principle about ethical rewards that one might call "ultra-Kantian," since even Kant himself rejected it.

Is it possible to defend a revelation without undermining the Revelation-Authority Principle? I believe that it is. The key is to develop criteria for the authenticity of the revelation that are independent of the content of the revelation. In the next chapter I shall argue that there are at least three such criteria: miracles, paradoxicality, and existential power. I shall have the most to say about the second, since I believe it has received less attention than the others. None of the three criteria are sufficient to provide proof of the authenticity of a revelation in the sense of proof demanded by classical foundationalist epistemology, nor do the three together provide such proof. They can, however, when taken together, be the ground of a reasonable faith.

---

22. Timothy P. Jackson, *The Priority of Love: Christian Charity and Social Justice* (Princeton: Princeton University Press, 2003), 81–89.
    23. Ibid., 89.

7

Criteria for a Genuine Revelation from God

In the last chapter I defended the claim that the contents of a genuine revelation from God should be believed because God has revealed them. This means that the criteria by which we recognize a genuine revelation from God should be somewhat independent of the contents of that revelation. There are at least three such criteria.

The Criterion of Miracles

One traditional way of defending a revelation's authenticity is to point to an accompanying miracle, with a miracle being understood as an event that must be the work of God. Such a miracle could be viewed as a "token" provided by God to show that a prophet does indeed have divine authority, much as an ancient messenger or herald of a king might carry a token provided by a king to attest the status of the messenger. I think it is clear that this traditional type of argument would, if successful, accomplish its goal without undermining the Revelation-Authority Principle, for in this case the authentication of the message is focused on the credentials of the messenger and not derived from the contents of the message itself.

And so it is not surprising that Christian thinkers defending the biblical revelation have time and time again appealed to accompanying miracles as authenticating the revelation. Aquinas says that the divine character of Scripture is attested by "works that surpass the ability of all nature."[1] Joseph Butler tells us that "as revelation is itself miraculous, all pretence to it must necessarily imply some pretence of miracles."[2] William Paley rhetorically asks about the function of miracles: "Now in what way can a revelation be made, but by miracles? In none which we are able to conceive."[3] More recently Richard Swinburne has appealed to the resurrection of Jesus as a "major authenticating miracle" that confirms both the claims of Jesus and the authority of the followers whom Jesus appointed to found his church.[4] One could, of course, also cite the impressive work of N. T. Wright on the resurrection as another attempt to defend miracles on behalf of the Christian revelation.[5]

Hume's Attack on Miracles

Of course, at least since the time of David Hume, the question of whether a miracle itself can be rationally believed has been controversial. As a result, the appeal to miracles as authenticating a revelation has become far less common. Those who think

1. *Summa Contra Gentiles* I, 6, 1.
2. Joseph Butler, *Analogy of Religion* (New York: E. P. Dutton, 1906), 203.
3. William Paley, *A View of the Evidences of Christianity* (New York: Robert Carter and Bros., 1854), 20–21.
4. Swinburne, *Revelation*, 95.
5. See N. T. Wright, *The Resurrection of the Son of God*, Christian Origins and the Question of God 3 (Minneapolis: Fortress, 2003).

that miracles (in the strong sense required by this use of the miraculous) cannot be rationally believed will not think this traditional criterion of the authenticity of a revelation can be used. However, in my view the force of the arguments of Hume and others against miracles has been vastly overestimated. The rhetorical influence of Hume's arguments is far greater than their logical force. This is, of course, a huge issue, and there is an enormous body of scholarly literature responding to Hume. I cannot possibly cover these issues here in the kind of depth deserved; that would call for at least a book-length study in its own right. Nevertheless, I need to say something about why Hume's arguments (and those of others) against miracles are less than decisive.[6]

Most readers see Hume's case against miracles as having two distinct elements. First, Hume offers a general argument that belief in a miracle would be unreasonable even if we had very strong testimony in support of the miracle. The heart of this argument is a claim that miracles are so inherently improbable that it is always more probable that a report of a miracle occurring is false than that the miracle actually took place. Second, he argues that the actual testimonial evidence in support of miracles is quite weak. One reason for this is that claims of miracles "are observed chiefly to abound among ignorant and barbarous nations." Hume says that when we examine the "first histories of all nations" we find ourselves "transported into a new world" in which ordinary natural processes are overwhelmed by "prodigies, omens, oracles." The reader of such histories is bound to wonder why "such prodigious events never happen in our days."[7]

6. For a somewhat fuller treatment of the issues, see C. Stephen Evans and R. Zachary Manis, *Philosophy of Religion: Thinking about Faith*, 2nd ed. (Downers Grove, IL: InterVarsity, 2009), 125–35.

7. David Hume, "Of Miracles," section 10 of *An Enquiry concerning Human Understanding* (Indianapolis: Hackett, 1993), 79–80.

How does Hume's first argument go? The starting point is his definition of a miracle as a *"transgression of a law of nature by a particular volition of the Deity, or by the interposition of some invisible agent."*[8] I shall ignore the last part of this definition since we are interested only in miracles as special acts of God that might be the basis of a revelation. I shall also ignore Hume's use of the word "transgression." The word is misleading, for if God does a miraculous act he does not transgress some principle that he ought to follow. Rather, I shall assume that by "transgression" Hume just means "exception." Thus understood, the definition captures one common conception of a miracle, that is, as an event God brings about that is exceptional in character, in that it does not seem to be the kind of event that purely natural causes can account for.

It is important not to think of a special act of God as some kind of "intervention" in which God comes in and acts in a world from which he is normally absent. As we saw in chapter 2, if God exists, then everything in the natural world depends on God not only for its beginning but also for its continued existence. God is responsible for the existence of the material world and the natural laws that govern the world's behavior. God is thus continually present in the natural order and is active within it. The laws of nature do not run "on their own" but hold because of God's continued activity. To say that a miracle involving an event that is an exception to the laws of nature is a special act of God is simply to say that God's actions in this case are indeed special. When God acts in a miraculous way, he does something unusual for a special purpose. To think otherwise is to adopt a deistic view of God and his relation to the natural world.

For Hume, this definition of a miracle as a special act of God that involves an exception to a law of nature implies that miracles must be extremely improbable, since he believes that

8. Ibid., 77n.

the probability of a type of event is determined by the frequency with which events of that type occur in our experience. Since the laws of nature describe what always happens unless a miracle occurs, miracles will be very rare and therefore must also be extremely improbable.[9] Miracles in this sense must be unusual events, for if we constantly observed what appeared to be an exception to a law of nature, we would quickly decide that the alleged law was not a true law of nature after all.

There are many weaknesses in Hume's argument. To begin, Hume only considers testimony in examining the evidence for miracles. However, there is no reason in principle why a person could not have firsthand experience of a miracle rather than having to rely on someone else's testimony. Physical evidence for a miracle could also be considered. Suppose, for example, that a person has been miraculously healed of cancer. Part of the evidence for this might consist of X-rays taken before and after the healing, first showing a tumor and then showing that the tumor has vanished. Of course, such evidence would still be partly reliant on testimony since we would need to trust that the radiologist is competent and has not confused the images. But almost all evidence requires relying on testimony in this weak sense.

A second major problem with Hume's argument has to do with his assumption that the probability of an event is simply a function of the frequency with which events of that type occur. It is easy to see that this principle is unsound as a general way of estimating probability. It is true that we do take into account in estimating probability how frequently an event of a certain

9. Some accuse Hume of begging the question against miracles because he claims that laws of nature describe what always happens. On this reading Hume is arguing that miracles never occur because they never occur, which is clearly a circular argument that assumes what it tries to show. Hume expresses himself a bit sloppily here, but I think it is reasonable to interpret him as intending to say what I say above. That at least is a charitable reading that still plausibly supports the conclusion Hume wants to defend.

type occurs, but that is far from the only thing we consider. Collisions between the earth and large meteorites, for example, are very rare indeed, and thus, measured by Hume's criterion of probability, such events must be extremely improbable. However, we have excellent evidence that they have occurred a few times in the past. Furthermore, if we detected a large meteorite coming toward the earth with the right (or, one might say, wrong) trajectory, the probability of a meteorite hitting the earth might approach certainty. It is true that, because such an event is rare, it is improbable that a large meteor will hit the earth tomorrow at 4:00 p.m.—at least it would be improbable if we had no evidence of a meteor approaching. However, even rare events do sometimes occur, and the probability that a meteor will hit the earth at some point during the earth's long history may be very high.

Hume's mistake is this. We do not estimate whether an event is probable purely by looking at the frequency with which events of that type occur. Rather, we take into account all we know about the situation. When we estimate the probability of a meteor hitting the earth, we take into account all we know about meteors: how many of them there are, what orbits the ones we know about follow, and so forth. Similarly, in estimating the probability of a miracle, we should not limit ourselves to considering how frequently miracles occur. Rather, we should take into account such facts as these: Is there a God? If there is a God, might God have reasons to perform a miracle?

Of course, if there is no God, and we know there is no God, the probability of a miracle might indeed be vanishingly low. However, we need good reason to believe that God does not exist. I have provided a case in chapters 2 through 5 that we do have evidence of something beyond the natural world: a God or gods. If that argument is sound, we would be rash to estimate the probability of a miracle as very low. Even if miracles do not happen every day, it might be highly probable that they occur at some times.

Do Miracles Still Occur?

So far I have been assuming for the sake of argument that Hume is right when he says that miracles are extremely rare events that no longer happen. However, both assumptions are dubious. Even if we agree with Hume that miracles, understood as exceptions to laws of nature, are somewhat uncommon, it is not clear that they are nearly as unusual as Hume thinks.

One might wonder whether Hume would have found reports of miracles quite so uncommon if he had left the streets of Enlightenment Edinburgh and talked with fishermen and farmers in the Scottish countryside. (Chesterton has a nice discussion of the credibility of accounts of the miraculous coming from ordinary uneducated people in *Orthodoxy*.)[10] Nevertheless, one can understand Hume's point here, especially when viewed against the backdrop of Catholic-Protestant polemics in the post-Reformation era. Many Protestant theologians, including the Scottish Presbyterians surrounding Hume, had adopted a "cessationist" view of miracles. To counter Catholic claims of healing miracles at the shrines of saints, Protestants had argued that miracles, though performed by God at the founding of the Christian church, no longer occur or at least are extremely rare.

Craig Keener has provided a powerful reply to this view of Hume's in his massive two-volume study, *Miracles: The Credibility of the New Testament Accounts*.[11] Keener shows how the whole debate is transformed if we reject the cessationism of Hume's theological contemporaries and also recognize the clear falsity of Rudolf Bultmann's famous dictum that "it is impossible

10. See G. K. Chesterton, *Orthodoxy* (Garden City, NY: Doubleday, 1959), 149–52.
11. Craig S. Keener, *Miracles: The Credibility of the New Testament Accounts*, 2 vols. (Grand Rapids: Baker Academic, 2011).

to use electrical light and the wireless and to avail ourselves of modern medical and surgical discoveries, and at the same time to believe in the New Testament world of spirits and miracles."[12] The fact is that in today's world there are hundreds of millions (if not billions) of people who believe in spirits and miracles *and* who cheerfully flip light switches and use "the wireless" (cell phones included). Such people may be confused or irrational, but they certainly exist. All this means that the debate about whether miracles happened in biblical times cannot and should not be divorced from the question of whether miracles happen today.

Keener's study includes literally hundreds of reports (selected from thousands) of credible eyewitness accounts of miracles. Many of these occur in what he calls the "recent West," thus clearly undermining Hume's assumption that miracle stories always come from "ignorant and barbarous tribes" in faraway times and places. However, even more of these reports come from the global South, and Keener has carefully collected, critically examined, and evaluated a mass of such claims from Africa, Asia, and South America. The miracle stories, many from highly educated people Keener personally knows, include healings from blindness, healings of those unable to walk, even resurrections from the dead and nature miracles.

Of course, different readers will approach the material with vastly different assumptions about what is possible and what is probable. However, for those willing to look at the evidence, many of the testimonies have the ring of sober truth. Here is one story, chosen more or less at random: A medical doctor named Tonye Briggs, currently practicing in Texas but working in Nigeria in the 1980s, had a female patient with such a serious condition that a colleague who was a gynecologist had to perform a tubal ligation. The woman prayed for healing during a healing crusade and three months later was found, by the

12. Rudolf Bultmann, *Kerygma and Myth* (New York: Harper and Row, 1961), 5.

same doctor who had removed her tubes, to be pregnant. The gynecologist could only marvel, "Your God is great." After the child's birth, a special X-ray confirmed that the woman had two healthy tubes, a test that was witnessed by Dr. Briggs.[13]

Keener thus demolishes two of the key assumptions behind Hume's argument. The first is Hume's assumption that the evidence for miracles is always testimonial evidence and never firsthand experience. Although Keener himself is offering us testimonies, it is clear that many of the people whose testimonies he reports do not accept Hume's assumption; they believe they have directly experienced miracles. The second assumption that Keener demolishes is Hume's claim that miracle stories only come from far-off times and places and from uneducated people. This claim was very likely false in Hume's own day, but it is clearly wrong today. As Keener himself puts it, the "a priori modernist assumption that genuine miracles are impossible is a historically and culturally conditioned premise. This premise is not shared by all intelligent or critical thinkers, and notably not by many people in non-Western cultures."[14]

A striking feature of the miracle accounts that Keener provides is that a great number of them occur at the time when the gospel is being introduced to a culture for the first time, and many have as one of their effects massive conversions and rapid church growth. The same is true time and time again, from India to China and the South Pacific to Africa. Although many of the stories, as one might expect, come from Pentecostal and neo-Pentecostal churches, a surprising number come from more traditional Protestant bodies as well as from Catholics, with experiences sometimes transforming the theological views of Western missionaries who had previously been prone to think that miracles no longer occur. If this seems to happen when the gospel is introduced to a culture

13. See Keener, *Miracles*, 1:326, for a fuller account of this episode.
14. See ibid., 2:764.

today, it certainly seems plausible to believe that it could have happened when God decided to found a church.

It may be tempting for some ethnocentric Westerners to dismiss the stories Keener tells that come from the global South, but it is a temptation that is the product of arrogance. The witnesses Keener summons are not ignorant or credulous people; they know very well that God does not always answer prayer and that miracles do not happen on demand. Their voices are ones we need to hear. If God is doing miracles today, then there is little reason to dogmatically hold that it was impossible for him to do miracles in the past.

What about arguments against miracles other than Hume's? I do not believe there are any such arguments that are strong. Sometimes it is alleged that miracles are simply incompatible with modern science. However, science and scientific laws describe what happens in the natural world. Questions about whether exceptions to those laws ever occur and, if so, whether these exceptions should be regarded as miracles, are not themselves scientific questions. No scientific experiments or observations could provide answers to these questions.

A critic of miracles might argue that it would be impossible to recognize an exception to a law of nature. If an apparent exception occurred, would it not be more reasonable to believe that some error in observation had occurred? (This is in essence another version of Hume's argument.) The answer is no, and that answer is required by science itself. One of the hallmarks of contemporary science is that scientific theories must be testable. It must be possible then to test alleged laws of nature to see if they are genuine laws of nature, and it is only through such testing that we could ever revise and improve our understanding of nature. If we always refused to consider whether any event was an exception to accepted laws of nature, we would no longer be able to test those laws.

The opponent of miracles might concede this point but argue that belief in miracles is still unreasonable. Yes, the opponent of miracles might say, we can and must recognize exceptions to what are accepted as the laws of nature. However, the opponent might go on to say, if we discover such an exception, we should believe not that a miracle has occurred but rather that our understanding of the laws of nature needs to be revised.

Richard Swinburne has given a powerful rejoinder to such a view.[15] Yes, it is possible that an observed exception to an accepted law of nature is evidence not that a miracle has occurred but that the law of nature we have previously accepted is false and should be revised. However, it would be dogmatic to insist that this will always be the case and that we can know a priori that miracles do not happen. Swinburne is surely right to say that if we decide that a law of nature should be revised on the basis of an apparent exception that has happened, the exception must be one that is repeatable. Laws of nature do not make reference to specific times and places. There is no plausible law of nature to the effect that "dead humans do not come back to life after three days except in first-century Palestine." If we find that an exception to a law of nature is not repeatable, it seems more reasonable to believe that an exception to the law has occurred than to believe that we should change our view about what the true laws of nature are.

This is particularly the case if the exceptional event happens in the right context. A freak event that cannot be scientifically explained might just be ignored as a freak event. However, suppose some individual claims to speak for God. How can we know that this person does indeed speak for God? If the individual has the power to do what only God could do and acts in ways

15. See Richard Swinburne, *The Concept of Miracle* (New York: Macmillan, 1971), and also Alvin Plantinga, "What Is 'Intervention'?," *Theology and Science* 6, no. 4 (2008): 369–401. For my own defense of miracles, see *Historical Christ*, 137–69.

that appear to involve exceptions to laws of nature, then these happenings would certainly provide support for the person's claims. This is especially true if the actions seem to manifest the character and purposes of a good and loving God, such as healings of those who are blind or lame and, preeminently, resurrection of the dead. I conclude that miracles are consistent with scientific knowledge, and a reasonable historian might well find that some miracles are adequately supported by evidence. If the revelation of God in Jesus is accompanied by miracles, this provides evidence that this revelation is a genuine revelation.

The Criterion of Paradoxicality

I turn now to the criterion of paradoxicality and here must look first to Kierkegaard. Kierkegaard was keenly aware of the need for criteria to distinguish a genuine revelation from spurious ones, given the existence of rival revelation claims. He was drawn to reflection on this issue partly by the case of Adolph Peter Adler, a Danish pastor who published a book of sermons in 1843, in the preface of which he claimed that Jesus had appeared to him and had dictated some of the sermons in the book. Kierkegaard thought this meant that Adler was claiming to possess something like apostolic authority, meaning by "apostle" not merely one of the original followers of Jesus but anyone who receives a direct revelation from Jesus that would give the bearer of the revelation a special authority. One might think of Adler's claim as similar to that of Paul, who also received his apostolic authority from a later appearance of Jesus. (Even though Adler's alleged appearance happened *much* later, Kierkegaard thinks that such quantitative differences cannot undermine qualitative similarities.)

Kierkegaard makes no use of the criterion of miracles because he thinks (mistakenly, in my view) that a person can believe in a miracle only if the person already possesses faith; the miracle cannot then be a support for faith. Having essentially given up on miracles as a criterion of an authentic revelation, Kierkegaard proposes several others that I have discussed in other places and that I think have limited value.[16] I believe, however, that Kierkegaard offers, implicitly at least, one other criterion for an authentic revelation that is more promising. I shall call this the criterion of paradoxicality.

Kierkegaard is well known, even infamous, for his claim that the incarnation, which he sees as the central element of Christian faith, is a paradox that human reason cannot understand or comprehend. Many commentators have understood his view as a claim that the incarnation involves a logical contradiction and that belief in the incarnation thus requires a repudiation of reason. I have argued at length that this interpretation is mistaken.[17] Space does not allow me to repeat those arguments here, but I think the interpretive case is powerful. Instead, I will merely lay out what I think Kierkegaard does mean by calling the incarnation "the absolute paradox."

First, the incarnation is definitely something that is "above" human reason, something that no human being can genuinely understand. In one sense, of course, the incarnation can be understood; to believe in the incarnation is to believe that Christ is both God and man. What cannot be understood is how this is possible, how an individual human being could be God, the almighty creator.

Why is it that humans cannot understand this? The primary reason is that we are finite beings and cannot understand God

16. For my discussion of this, see "Kierkegaard on Religious Authority: The Problem of the Criterion," in *Kierkegaard on Faith and the Self* (Waco: Baylor University Press, 2006), 239–62.

17. See, e.g., my *Passionate Reason: Making Sense of Kierkegaard's* Philosophical Fragments (Bloomington: Indiana University Press, 1992) and *Kierkegaard's* Fragments *and* Postscript: *The Religious Philosophy of Johannes Climacus* (1983; repr., Amherst, NY: Humanity Books, 1999).

or what God is able to do. When we try to conceive of the God-man, we find it impossible to do so; to us it seems impossible or at the very least immensely improbable for God to become a human being.[18] However, this inability says more about our cognitive limitations than it does about God's power.

Besides thinking that the incarnation is "above" human reason, Kierkegaard also thinks that there is a natural tension between God's self-revelation through the incarnation and human ways of thinking. Humans are sinful, and our actual reasoning is heavily influenced by our sinfulness. Our sinfulness manifests itself both in pridefulness and in selfishness. Both qualities make belief in the incarnation difficult. Because of pride, we have a natural tendency to regard as "absurd" what we cannot understand. Because of selfishness, we have no experience of completely self-giving love, and yet the actions of a God who needs nothing from us but became incarnate for our salvation could be motivated only by self-giving love. We therefore have a natural tendency to be skeptical about such love and the actions it inspires. For these reasons, Kierkegaard says that the incarnation is not only an insoluble mystery for humans but also something humans have a natural inclination to disbelieve. In his words, the incarnation always carries with it "the possibility of offense." It offends us by insulting our prideful self-sufficiency and by showing us, in contrast with God's self-giving love, how selfish we are.

So far it might appear that paradoxicality is a negative factor in assessing the incarnation. Surprisingly, however, Kierkegaard does not see things this way. He views the paradoxicality of the incarnation, and even the fact that it poses the possibility of offense, as signs that this is a genuine revelation from God. In

---

18. For example, Kierkegaard calls the incarnation "the most improbable of all things" and "the strangest thing of all." See Søren Kierkegaard, *Philosophical Fragments*, trans. Edna H. Hong and Howard V. Hong (Princeton: Princeton University Press, 1985), 52, 101.

chapter 3 of *Philosophical Fragments*, Kierkegaard (through the voice of his pseudonym Johannes Climacus) gives an extended account of the incarnation as paradoxical. He follows this chapter with an appendix in which he discusses offense, arguing that the fact that some people are offended by the incarnation is actually "an indirect proof of the correctness of the paradox."[19]

This appendix, which is subtitled "An Acoustical Illusion," describes a kind of extended conversation between the incarnation, personified as "the Paradox," and the human understanding, which is also personified. As we will see, the conversation quickly turns negative and can aptly be described as a name-calling contest. When a person is offended by the incarnation, the understanding sees itself as having made a discovery that justifies a negative judgment on the incarnation. The understanding accuses the Paradox of being "the Absurd." The Paradox, however, takes a different view of the matter. The judgment that human reason makes about the Paradox is not an original discovery of reason at all but part of the content of the revelation. In effect, the Paradox claims that the alleged "discovery" of reason is simply an echo (acoustical illusion) of what the Paradox teaches about itself:

> The understanding has not discovered this; on the contrary, it was the Paradox that ushered the understanding to the wonder stool and replies: Now what are you so surprised about? It is just as you say, but the surprising thing is that you think that what you say is an objection, but the truth in the mouth of a hypocrite is dearer to me than to hear it from an angel and an apostle.[20]

Human reason calls the Paradox "the Absurd," but the Paradox replies, in effect, by claiming that this is not an objection

19. Ibid., 51. Translation modified.
20. Ibid., 52. I have again modified the Hong translation.

at all but simply an echo (somewhat distorted, as echoes are) of what the Paradox claims about itself. Whether reason tries to "help" by an attempt to reinterpret and explain the Paradox or simply denounces the Paradox, it is in both cases powerless. The Paradox "refuses to put up with" reason's attempts to explain it, though it is not surprised at this behavior: "For is that not what philosophers are for—to make supernatural things ordinary and trivial?" When the understanding is offended and denounces the Paradox, the Paradox calmly interprets this behavior as evidence that the Paradox is a genuine revelation of God.

On my interpretation, then, offense is a product of two factors: the fact that human thinking cannot understand how an incarnation is possible combined with the fact that humans, as prideful and selfish beings, have a natural tendency to reject what they cannot understand, especially if what they cannot understand presents itself as motivated by a kind of love we humans do not exhibit ourselves and have no other experience of. One might say that the response of human reason in this case is precisely what one would predict would be the case if the facts are as the revelation claims. However, if a hypothesis predicts some consequence and that consequence occurs, that is evidence for the hypothesis. The gospel includes as part of its content a prediction that human reason will have a tendency to denounce it as absurd. If that is the case, it appears that the natural response of humans to the incarnation is evidence that the incarnation is a genuine revelation from God.

It is important to recognize that although Kierkegaard thinks there is a natural tendency for human reason to reject the incarnation, this tendency is by no means one that makes such a rejection inevitable. Rather, he stresses that it is possible for the understanding and the Paradox to come together in a happy relationship; this happy relationship is called "faith." Faith and offense are said to be analogous to happy and unhappy erotic

love, respectively, and the relationship between the human understanding and God's revelation is claimed to be analogous to the
relationship between self-love and love.[21] In a happy love affair,
self-love transcends itself; it is dethroned by love but, paradoxi-
cally, fulfilled in that the person in love finds true happiness in
seeking the happiness of the beloved. However, the person who
is mired in selfishness "shrinks from erotic love" and can neither
understand it nor dare to love.[22] Such a selfish person typically
becomes embittered by love. Similarly, Kierkegaard thinks that
a person who has the happy passion of faith actually finds that
her reason is fulfilled when she believes that which surpasses
the power of reason. The person who dismisses that which she
cannot fully understand is rejecting this fulfillment.

The paradoxicality of the incarnation is then no barrier to
faith, at least not as Kierkegaard sees things. To the contrary,
it seems to be a mark of the genuineness of the revelation. One
might think that Kierkegaard's views about revelation are eccen-
tric, but I believe there are at least hints of a similar view in the
famous Catholic theologian and philosopher Thomas Aquinas.
The ground of this is Aquinas's view that a true revelation from
God would include truths that surpass the ability of human
reason to discover and that a revelation that did not include such
truths would give us a false picture of God, since we know God
truly only "when we believe him to be above everything that it
is possible for man to think about him."[23] This seems to imply
at the very least that any genuine revelation from God would
include things that humans would find surprising.

However, Aquinas goes further than merely saying that the
Christian revelation contains things that are surprising; he says
that it contains things that we naturally find hard to believe: "In

21. Ibid., 48.
22. Ibid.
23. *Summa Contra Gentiles* I, 5, 3.

this faith there are truths preached that surpass every human intellect; the pleasures of the flesh are curbed; it is taught that the things of the world should be spurned."[24] After this description of the Christian revelation, Aquinas makes the surprising claim that for humans to believe such things is itself "the greatest of miracles," which seems to imply that there is a very strong natural tendency not to believe them. However, Aquinas, like Kierkegaard, treats this natural tendency toward disbelief as a confirmation of the genuineness of the revelation.

These hints are confirmed by Aquinas's treatment of Islamic revelation claims. One of his criticisms is that Muhammad "did not bring forth any signs produced in a supernatural way, which alone fittingly gives witness to divine inspiration."[25] However, he also criticizes Islam because he thinks its revelation lacks the off-putting character of the Christian revelation. Instead, he thinks the Islamic revelation panders to base human desires; Muhammad "seduced the people by promises of carnal pleasure to which the concupiscence of the flesh goads us," and "his teaching also contained precepts that were in conformity with his promises," thus giving "free rein to carnal pleasure."[26] In effect, Aquinas thinks that Islam proclaims truths that people have a natural desire to believe. One might conclude that, if Aquinas is right, Islam lacks an important characteristic of a genuine revelation, which calls for us to believe things that we do not understand and have difficulty believing.[27] I conclude

24. *Summa Contra Gentiles* I, 6, 1.
25. *Summa Contra Gentiles* I, 6, 4.
26. *Summa Contra Gentiles* I, 6, 4. Aquinas also seems to anticipate another of Kierkegaard's criteria of authentic revelation, the "no worldly means" criterion, when he accuses Muhammad of relying on "the power of his arms—which are signs not lacking even to robbers and tyrants."
27. I make no judgment here about whether Aquinas is fair to Islam in these comments. One might note on behalf of Islam that some Muslim apologists argue that the fact that the illiterate Muhammad produced the Qur'an is itself a great miracle, thus providing good evidence for the authenticity of the revelation. Muslim apologists also sometimes argue that polytheism is the natural belief of humans and thus

that Aquinas agrees with Kierkegaard that what I have called paradoxicality is an important criterion of a genuine revelation. A genuine revelation from God would contain elements that are surprising, impossible to fully understand, and difficult to believe.

Distinguishing between the Paradoxical and the Bizarre

There is an obvious objection to the idea of paradoxicality as a criterion of a genuine revelation: even if one concedes that a genuine revelation would contain elements that are surprising and paradoxical, and also that there would be a natural human tendency to disbelieve such a revelation, one might think that these facts can hardly be helpful in recognizing a genuine revelation. Much that is proposed to humans for belief is simply bizarre and crazy, and even some alleged divine revelations seem to fit into this category. That an alleged revelation strikes us as bizarre and crazy is therefore surely not a strong point in favor of that revelation. In fact, one might argue that the plethora of absurd religious claims means that paradoxicality is a negative quality rather than a point in favor of an alleged revelation.

Suppose, for example, that someone claimed that God had become incarnate as a frog rather than as a human being. This seems to be even more absurd than the claim that God became a human being, and thus more paradoxical. One might respond to this by claiming that a frog incarnation would be not just paradoxical but downright bizarre. I think this response is exactly right, and it shows the need to distinguish what is paradoxical from what is bizarre. The paradoxicality that is linked to a genuine revelation must be a special kind of paradoxicality, one that allows us to distinguish between the quality a genuine

---

that the Qur'an, in teaching monotheism, does urge humans to believe what they do not find easy to believe.

divine revelation would possess and mere bizarreness or weird-
ness. But how can this be done?

Here is a first stab: the paradoxicality that is present in a
genuine revelation should be an *initial* paradoxicality. A genuine
revelation from God would seem paradoxical at first. However,
the qualities that seem initially paradoxical ought to be such
that a person of good will could later, on reflection, see that
these are exactly the qualities one would expect to find in a
genuine revelation from God. In order to see this the person
must undergo a transformation. The person goes from thinking "no way" to saying, "Why of course." This is precisely how
both Kierkegaard and Aquinas seem to see things. For both
Kierkegaard and Aquinas, the change in belief appears to make
perfect sense in hindsight. What, if anything, can we say about
this transformation? To make sense of this important change, I
need to move to the third criterion for an authentic revelation,
what I shall call the criterion of existential power.

The Criterion of Existential Power

When a person changes from seeing a revelation as improbable
or even absurd to seeing it as true or even certainly true, the
change cannot be accounted for simply in terms of the acquisi-
tion of new evidence. The case is similar in some ways to what
occurs in a scientific revolution, as described by such thinkers
as Thomas Kuhn.[28] Prior to the revolution the scientists have
a body of background beliefs, given which no amount of new
evidence will make the theories of the new paradigm probable.
Furthermore, although there are some problems and tensions
with the prevailing scientific "paradigm," scientists do have ways
of explaining the problems and dealing with the recalcitrant

---

28. See Thomas Kuhn, *The Structure of Scientific Revolutions* (Chicago: University
of Chicago Press, 1970).

data. For example, all the observed motions of the planets understood in accordance with Ptolemy as revolving around the earth can be explained by the Ptolemaic system. Hence, from the earlier perspective, the new beliefs seem irrational, even paradoxical.

After the scientific revolution, however, the new perspective seems perfectly reasonable. What has happened is not just that new evidence has been acquired; rather, the scientists have adopted a new set of background beliefs that alter what is viewed as evidence and how the evidence is weighted. Interestingly, philosophers of science borrow from the language of religion to describe this phenomenon; they call it "radical conversion." We might say that it is the scientists themselves who have changed; their view of the world has been transformed. This change, however, is not one that can be described in terms of standard accounts of evidence and probability theory. The change is not just that the scientists have new evidence. Rather, they have changed their view of what counts as evidence.

In a similar way, I believe that the change from seeing a revelation as improbable or paradoxical to seeing it as plausible or even definitely true must involve a transformation of the person who is encountering the revelation. The person is exposed to new content and given evidence that the revelation is genuine. But in addition to this, the one who encounters the revelation becomes radically different—so different that we could say he or she has become a new person, has been born again.

To such a person the Christian story, which centers on God becoming a human being to rescue him or her from sin and death, is not just a strange or bizarre claim, no matter how impossible it would have been for a human to invent such an idea. The person who has been converted, or who is in the process of being converted, comes to understand that the story is one that offers precisely what humans need. The revelation tells me who I am, what my true condition is, and how that condition can be transformed. I come to see that the key fits the lock, and the whole story takes on the ring of truth.

This is, I think, the truth that lies behind the claim of Reformed epistemologists that we come to know the truth of the gospel not simply by acquiring evidence but through the internal testimony of the Holy Spirit. The Holy Spirit's work in our lives is not simply a matter of giving us a certain kind of evidence; it is also a matter of the Spirit transforming us into the kinds of beings who can see the evidence and interpret it properly. Part of the evidence that the person can now see will include things such as the following: I now recognize that I am a sinful being and that this is the root of my problems. I can also see that the remedy offered by the gospel is precisely what is needed to remedy my condition. Only God himself could save me, but to do that God needed to assume the human condition himself. Prior to this change in perception, I may well have thought that the very idea of a person being God was simply unbelievable. Now, however, I can see that the story of the incarnation is exactly what is needed.

As I begin to think about the possibility that my prior ways of thinking may be limited and short-sighted, it may occur to me that the very implausibility of the story (to my previous self) is part of what makes it seem true. Once I understand my own selfishness and pride, I will mistrust those prideful and selfish reactions. Why should I expect God's actions to be limited to what I can understand? Why shouldn't a God who wishes to save me be a God who is moved by a kind of love I have never myself given or even experienced?

It seems entirely proper that the process by which we come to know God truly and relate to God properly be one that involves fundamental transformation on our part. For God wants us not merely to come to know the truth about him but to learn that truth through a process by which we become the kind of people who are capable of loving and serving God. But when that transformation has happened, or at least when it has begun, everything looks different. We look at the evidence differently, and the transformation in our own lives is itself a kind of evidence. Thus, the third and final criterion of an authentic revelation is the existential power of that revelation.

The essential role of God's Spirit thus does imply that the decision to accept a revelation is not simply a matter of evidence in the ordinary sense. But it does not imply that evidence is unimportant, since one of the outcomes of the witness of the Spirit may be that we are changed in ways that enable us to view the evidential situation rightly, including even ordinary evidence that we may have been unable to appreciate. The power of the Spirit to change the way we view things is well expressed in this entry from Kierkegaard's journal on the problem of the historical reliability of the Gospel narratives:

> One who truly believes that Christ was and is God (here is the main impact of offense), who prays to him repeatedly every day, who finds all his joy in association with him and in thinking of him—such a person does indeed come to terms with the historical. How silly to be upset if one gospel-writer said one thing and a second another; he can turn to Christ in prayer and say: This disturbs me, but is it not true that you still are and remain with me? It is nonsense that the significance of historical details should be decisive with respect to faith in Him who is present with one and with whom one speaks daily and to whom one turns. . . .
>
> Believe that Christ is God—then call upon him, pray to him, and the rest comes by itself. When the fact that he is present is more intimately and inwardly certain than all historical information—then you will come out all right with the details of his historical existence—whether the wedding was at Cana

or perhaps somewhere else, whether there were two disciples or only one.[29]

Conclusion

All three of the criteria I have discussed are important. God gives miraculous signs to show that a revelation is authentic. The content of the revelation should be something that humans could never have discovered on their own, yet something that when revealed makes sense of the human condition in a way that no human philosophy could. Both the recognition of the miracles and the understanding of the paradoxical content require that the encounter with the revelation be personally transformative. The ultimate response to the New Atheism must include our own personal testimony to the work of God in our lives. That is something that all Christians should understand, and it is certainly deeply embedded in the evangelical wing of Christianity.

29. *Kierkegaard's Papirer*, VIII[1] A 565, in *Søren Kierkegaard's Journals and Papers*, trans. and ed. Edna H. Hong and Howard V. Hong (Bloomington: Indiana University Press, 1967), entry 318, 1:133.

8

Conclusions

MAKING THE CASE FOR CHRISTIAN FAITH

We began by looking at the strident case that the New Atheists make against religious belief in general and Christian belief in particular. Part of their case against religious belief is that religion has a pernicious impact on society as well as on individuals. This is a charge that has been well addressed by others, and I have not attempted to answer it in this book. Instead I have chosen to focus on what I see as the core accusation of the New Atheists: that religious faith is irrational because it is not based on evidence. Even the accusation that religious faith is pernicious is closely linked to this core charge, because one of the alleged sins of religious belief is that it corrodes our rational faculties, giving us a disposition to believe what we have no reason to believe is true.

Natural Signs for God Revisited

The case I have made for the reasonableness of Christian faith is a version of the classical "two-stage" type of account. The first stage is an argument that belief in God is justified. This stage of the argument could be supported by Muslims, non-Christian Jews, and other theists, since its goal is simply to argue that it is reasonable to believe in a God or gods who transcend the natural order. If there were a being like this who wanted to be in relationship with humans, we would expect that God to provide evidence that was widely accessible to ordinary people, and we would expect to find that most people throughout human history and in many different cultures have believed in a God or gods. And that is exactly what we find to be the case. Every human culture seems to include belief in God or gods as a common element, and today even secular psychologists and cognitive scientists are increasingly convinced that humans are "hardwired" toward religious belief. The resilience of faith is demonstrated, for example, by the presence of strong faith communities in the former Soviet Union and China in spite of the decades of indoctrination against religious belief.

This does not mean that most humans believe in God on the basis of "proofs" or logical arguments. Rather, belief is triggered by "natural signs." God has placed these pointers to himself in human experience, along with a tendency to respond to the signs by forming beliefs in God. However, though belief in God does not have to be based on argument, it is possible to become reflectively aware of the signs and then to develop the signs into arguments, and that is what has happened with the classical arguments for God's existence. In that case we have propositional evidence for God's reality. However, even those believers who do not engage in such arguments may still be said to base their beliefs in God on evidence that is nonpropositional in character.

The first natural sign we examined is the basic sense of wonder that there is a universe at all, a wonder that creates a natural tendency to think that our universe is something that might never have been. Its very existence is a mystery that cries out for some answer beyond itself. This sign is the basis of what philosophers call the "cosmological argument."

The second sign we examined is our natural perception of the world as embodying purposiveness. All around us we see aspects of nature that seem to fit together to serve some good end, whether that end is the functioning of human bodily organs such as the eyes or the lungs or the beauty seen in sunsets and mountains and beaches. Our sense that the natural world is purposive is so strong that even advertisers rely on it; shampoo makers, for example, claim their products will work well because they are "natural."

Contrary to what New Atheists claim, there is no reason to think that the force of this second sign is undermined by the fact that the order we see in nature is the result of an evolutionary process. God is the creator of the whole of nature and all of its processes, so the fact that something occurs as the result of a natural process does not mean it is not God's doing. God is not a finite entity among other entities. God is not just "one more thing" within the natural order but the source of the whole natural order. It follows from this that God and the natural order are not two rival hypotheses that mutually exclude each other, such that if God does something, nature is not involved. It is a mistake to think that what comes about by natural causes is not the result of God's creative activity.[1] The purposive order we see in nature is real and not an illusion, regardless of how God brought it about.

1. It is true that in my discussion of miracles I looked at miracles as events that cannot be fully explained by natural causes, and I claimed that this characteristic is a sign of God's special involvement. However, this does not mean that God is normally not active in creation or that his actions are limited to miracles. Rather, we must remember that the whole of nature is the outcome of God's activity all the time. A miracle is not an "intervention" in which God steps into a natural order from which he is normally absent. Rather, a miracle represents a special act of God. God is the source of all natural processes; when acting miraculously God simply causes nature to behave differently than the way he ordinarily causes it to behave.

If the evolutionary story is true, this actually provides even more reason to believe in God, for it means that the beneficial order we see in nature is the result of a still deeper kind of order; all of it is the result of amazingly intricate, "fine-tuned" laws, which look very much as if they have been orchestrated to make possible living things and all the other things we see as valuable.

When we look within ourselves, we find other natural signs that are even more powerful. We humans are aware of moral obligations, laws that are not the result of any human legislator but that we recognize ourselves as obliged to live up to. Morally sensitive people see themselves as in some way accountable or responsible for how they live, even if they cannot explain to whom they are accountable. Thus even people who are atheists may have some awareness of God, who is constantly addressing them through conscience—though of course they do not recognize what they are hearing as really the voice of God, and to be sure, they hear God's voice as filtered and shaped by culture.

Another clear sign that points to God is found in human nature itself. Humans are certainly animals, creatures who are part of the natural order. Nevertheless, we recognize that human persons have a unique status within that order, a kind of dignity or inherent value that implies that human persons should be treated with respect. Even secular documents, such as the United Nations' Declaration on Human Rights, recognize that humans have a special status. As persons, humans have not only the value other animals have but also a unique value that is inherent in who we are and does not simply derive from what we have accomplished. From the standpoint of Judaism and Christianity, this is a recognition that human persons are made in God's image. God is the ultimate Good and the source of all that is good. Anything that is made in God's image is therefore a sign that points back to the creator.

Of course, these signs do not amount to proofs in the sense that they would convince any reasonable person who considers them. However, they do have the Pascalian characteristics I argued would be expected in evidence for God. They are easily resistible; those who do not want to believe in God can certainly discount them or explain them away. However, they are also widely accessible, evidence that just about any person can recognize and that even unbelievers often acknowledge as having genuine force.

I do not believe that these signs give us adequate or reliable knowledge of what God is like. The variety of views of God found among human cultures is evidence of that. To really know God we must hear from God and have a relationship with God. However, these natural signs should at least unsettle the dogmatic naturalist who is sure that there is nothing beyond the natural world. They provide support for anti-naturalism and therefore ought to make us curious as to whether it is possible to discover more about what is beyond the natural world. They should put us "on alert" to find out whether whatever is beyond the natural world has communicated with us.

Believing God's Self-Revelation

Christianity proclaims that we can know God and relate to God because God has revealed himself in human history. I have argued that there are three criteria by which we could recognize an authentic revelation: miracles, paradoxicality, and existential power. In this chapter I shall argue that all three of these criteria are fulfilled by the Bible and thus that it is reasonable to recognize the Bible as God's revelation. First, the prophets and apostles who gave us the Bible performed miracles as signs that they indeed spoke for God. In particular, Jesus of Nazareth, who is the central focus of the Bible, was raised by God from the dead so as to show that he was indeed someone who spoke for God.

Someone might well think at this point that I have moved too quickly. Aren't there a lot of other sacred writings found in the world's great religions? Aren't there stories of miracles found in these religions as well? Interestingly, when one examines the sacred writings of the great religions, the Christian claims turn out to be highly unusual. It is in fact quite rare to find a sacred book that is put forward as containing a revelation *that ought to be believed on the grounds that it has been revealed by God.* For example, take the sacred writings of Buddhism, such as the Tripitaka, a vast collection of writings sometimes known as the Pali Canon because of the language in which they were originally written. Neither Gautama (the Buddha) nor Buddhists see these writings as a revelation from God that ought to be believed because the contents have been revealed. On the contrary, Buddhists claim that the truths contained in these sacred writings can be grasped by human reason and ought to be believed because they can be seen to be true, not because they have been revealed.

Something similar could be said about the sacred texts revered by Hindus. There are, of course, many revered writings, the oldest of which are collectively known as the Vedas. These writings certainly have authoritative status for Hindus, but they do not have that status because they are regarded as a revelation from God that must be believed for that reason. Rather, they are regarded as a storehouse of spiritual truths that have been discovered by sages. Something very similar could be said about the revered writings of such ancient Chinese traditions as Confucianism and Taoism.

If one looks at the great religions of the world, it is only the Qur'an that seems to provide a genuine rival to the Christian claim to possess a revelation from God. Devout Muslims believe this book to be the very words of God revealed to Muhammad. Interestingly, Muslims also accept the Christian revelation as one that comes from God and regard Jesus as an important prophet of God, though they believe that the Christian revelation is marred by error at points and that Muhammad is the supreme prophet of God. So how does the Qur'an measure up when evaluated by the three criteria discussed in the last chapter?

Interestingly, Muslims do not claim that their sacred book was authenticated by miracles. Muhammad did not in fact claim to perform miracles. Instead, Muslims claim that the Qur'an is itself a miracle. Its profundity and deep truth is so clear that no external criteria are necessary. I can see how such an argument could be convincing to those who have been formed by such a book and have been taught to revere it since childhood. However, my own view is that it is not possible to discern the divine origins of a book as a special, authoritative revelation merely by recognizing it as a book that contains profound truths. There are many books from China, India, and other cultures that appear to contain deep and profound truths, and the same is true of the Bible. The fact that a book meets this standard does not provide strong evidence for thinking it is a special, authoritative revelation.

Actually, just the opposite might be the case. In the last chapter I argued that one of the characteristics of a genuine revelation from God would be that it contains truths we humans could not figure out for ourselves. If one of the characteristics one should expect to see in a true revelation from God is paradoxicality, then this is another difficulty for Islam. Even if it is true that when we read a book we recognize it as containing truths, this does not show that those truths are ones God has revealed so that we will believe them. Rather, we might expect what God has revealed to be something we could never have discovered on our own, even something we have difficulty understanding and believing.

The Christian revelation is thus essentially the only plausible candidate among the great religions' sacred writings to be a special revelation from God with the credentials we would expect such a revelation to possess. It is thus well worth considering whether those credentials hold up under inspection. I shall briefly discuss this by looking at each of the three characteristics we would expect to find in a genuine revelation from God.

The Miracle of the Resurrection

Christians have always maintained that their faith stands or falls with the resurrection of Jesus of Nazareth from the dead. In one of the earliest Christian documents, the apostle Paul affirms that "if Christ has not been raised, your faith is futile; you are still in your sins" (1 Cor. 15:17). Certainly, raising someone from the dead would seem to be the kind of authenticating miracle that would give one assurance that someone who claims to be a prophet really does speak with divine authority. If Christ was raised from the dead, then we have good reason to think that he was at least a person who has for us a message from God. (Christians, of course, believe that Christ is more than this, but certainly he is at least this.)

Are there good reasons to believe that Christ was indeed raised from the dead? The nature of history precludes anything like a mathematical proof of such a thing. Historical sources can always be doubted; reinterpretations of what has happened are always possible. However, this situation is in itself not surprising or worrying. We saw when we looked at the natural signs for God's existence that God would be expected to give the kind of evidence that does not compel belief but gives room for the person who does not want to know God to explain that evidence away. We would expect something like that to be true in the case of the evidence for a revelation as well. God wants humans to serve him freely. He is not interested in "followers" who were conscripted into his army against their will. One would expect clear evidence for such a momentous claim, but both for theological reasons and because of the nature of history, nothing like absolute proof should be looked for.

I am not a historian or biblical scholar, and the historical case for belief in the resurrection of Jesus has been better explained by scholars who do have such expertise.[2] However, it is worth looking at the evidence that is available from a layperson's point of view. Much of the evidence is testimonial in character. In the Epistles of Paul as well as the four Gospels, there is clear testimony that Jesus was raised from the dead. These witnesses tell us that the tomb in which Jesus had been placed (that of a prominent figure) was empty and also that Jesus appeared to multiple people on multiple occasions after his resurrection.

It is the very nature of testimonial evidence that whether the testimony is believed depends partly on how trustworthy the witnesses appear, which to a certain extent is a matter of listening carefully and deciding whether the witness seems to care about the truth. In the case of the Gospels there are good reasons to trust the testimony.

One reason is that the testimony comes from a time quite close to the events. In the nineteenth century it became popular for critics of the biblical narrative to claim that the Gospels and other New Testament writings must have been written much later than the events they claim happened. After all, thought the critics, these stories about the resurrection and other miracles are obviously legends, and it usually takes quite a long time for legends of this sort to develop. (An obvious parallel would be the legends about the Buddha, most of which clearly come

2. For a detailed statement of the historical evidence, albeit still presented in an accessible form, see William Lane Craig, *Historical Evidence for the Resurrection of Jesus* (Eugene, OR: Wipf and Stock, 2000).

from a period hundreds of years later than Gautama lived.) So it was thought that the books of the New Testament must be from the second century AD or even later.

Unfortunately for those critics, all this speculation turned out to be wrong.[3] Virtually all historical scholars now agree that the Epistles of Paul are the earliest books of the New Testament and that Paul's writings originated no later than twenty-five to thirty-five years after Jesus's death. The four Gospels themselves are somewhat later, but not nearly as late as the skeptical critics imagined. There is some disagreement over the dating, but most scholars now think Mark is the earliest Gospel, most likely written in about 60 AD, with Matthew and Luke a few years later, and John the latest, written in about 95 AD. (A later date for John is implausible since a fragment of the Gospel was found in Egypt dating from about 130 AD; the Gospel would have to have been written, copied, and transmitted to Egypt well before this.) So the first three Gospels were written within thirty to forty-five years of the death of Jesus, during a period when eyewitnesses and people who had known eyewitnesses were still alive. There was little time for legends to accumulate.

A second reason to trust the witnesses in this case stems from their motivation. We tend to discount testimony when the person who is telling us the story stands to profit if we believe the story. However, if someone tells me something that is likely to be costly to the witness, that is a strong point in favor of believing the testimony. It is clear that the disciples of Jesus and other early followers had little to gain from making up a story about Jesus's resurrection. On the contrary, by telling their story they faced persecution and exclusion from the surrounding culture. They not only risked death on the basis of the truth

3. For a good summary of the historical story, see Stephen Neill and N. T. Wright, *The Interpretation of the New Testament, 1861–1986*, 2nd ed. (Oxford: Oxford University Press, 1988).

of the story; many of them actually suffered death because of their witness. It is hard to imagine them being willing to do so unless they were convinced of the truth of Jesus's resurrection.

This leads to another reason to believe these witnesses. Unless Jesus was really raised from the dead, it is hard to account for the transformation of the apostles and other early followers of Jesus. After all, Jesus had been executed by the Romans as a criminal. His followers, who had hoped he would be the Messiah who would liberate Israel from the Romans, were understandably demoralized. What changed them from a secretive, fearful group to a bold community of people who started a movement that quickly transformed the entire Roman world?

These early followers of Jesus very quickly came to view Jesus as more than human. The earliest Christian communities, insofar as we can know about them through Paul's letters, already worshiped Jesus as divine. This in itself is astonishing since the earliest followers were all Jews, strict monotheists who would have been expected to think that any human claim to divinity was a form of blasphemy. Many controversies swirl in Paul's early churches, and these controversies show up clearly in the letters, but Paul never seems to have had to defend the exalted status of Christ. It was not a point of controversy. It was something that was already an established truth for those early churches. Again, it is hard to imagine anything less than the resurrection of Jesus that would account for this amazing view of Jesus's status.

Of course, it is not the mere fact that Jesus was raised from the dead that led these early Christians to believe he was God. Rather, the resurrection was a sign that Jesus's own teaching about himself should be believed. Even if one is skeptical about whether Jesus really taught that he was divine, it is clear that some of Jesus's actions, such as forgiving sins, implied a claim to divinity. The resurrection was a sign that Jesus could be believed.

The last reason to trust these witnesses is that they seem to be honest people who want to get things right. Many of the details of the stories in the Gospels actually appear to be somewhat embarrassing and awkward for the early church. One good example is the baptism of Jesus by John the Baptist, an episode that could be read as giving John more status than Jesus. John had disciples of his own who were independent of Jesus's followers and to some degree provided a rival community that could have undermined the early Christian movement. Yet it is clearly recorded by the Gospels. There are quite a few other episodes that have this same character. Even those scholars who are highly skeptical of the four Gospels tend to accept at least those parts of the Gospels that are regarded as embarrassing in this way, since it seems implausible that such stories would be made up by Christ's followers.

However, we should ask ourselves why these awkward or embarrassing stories were included by the writers. I can think of only two possible reasons. One is that the writers were honest people who were trying to tell the story as it happened. If someone is willing to share information with me that reflects badly on the person or the person's community, then that witness is pretty trustworthy. The other is that the historical truth about Jesus was so well known by so many people at the time the Gospels were written that the writers were forced to include these stories in order to be credible. On the basis of either of these suppositions (or both), the historical credibility of the Gospels is high.

However, a critic might protest, aren't there contradictions in the accounts given by the four Gospels, and don't those differences undermine their historical reliability? Actually, differences in testimony can be a sign that the testimony is honest and not a made-up story. In a criminal case, some differences in testimony between eyewitnesses to a crime are to be expected. In fact, witnesses' stories agreeing too closely would be suspicious, a sign that the witnesses have colluded and agreed on what to say. In any case, there is no question that there is a basic consistency in the picture the Gospel writers give of Jesus and his death and resurrection. If that were not the case, the early church would not have accepted all four as genuine.

In looking at the question of the historical reliability of the Gospels, it is important to understand what ancient people understood as historical reliability. Of course, there were no tape recorders or video cameras. Ancient people understood that when a historian or biographer recorded a speech that was made, the account would not be a verbatim transcript but rather would convey the gist of what was said. The Gospel writers clearly selected materials, interpreted their selections to emphasize certain themes and points, and felt free to rearrange the order of events so as to make the story meaningful and memorable for their intended audiences. These were common practices among ancient historians. Many of the "contradictions" critics find in the Gospels simply reflect these practices. In affirming the reliability of the Gospels, I mean to say that someone who reads them will get a truthful picture of the kind of person Jesus was, of the kinds of things he did and said. Furthermore, they will be given powerful reasons to believe that Jesus of Nazareth, crucified by the Romans, rose from the dead. His tomb was empty, and he appeared to his followers.

The Paradoxicality of the Story

How does the Christian revelation fare when judged by the second criterion we examined in the last chapter, that of paradoxicality? I argued there that a true revelation from God would likely seem initially implausible though in retrospect would make sense. The Christian thinker who has said the most about the paradoxicality of the Christian revelation is the nineteenth-century Danish philosopher Søren Kierkegaard, so it seems fitting to see what Kierkegaard has to say about the matter.

For Kierkegaard the heart of the Christian revelation lies in the claim that Jesus of Nazareth is God incarnate. Although fully human, Jesus is also God. Kierkegaard provides no theory as to how this is possible. In fact, he stresses that the belief that Jesus was the "God-man" is a mystery that human reason cannot unravel. We cannot really understand how this is possible. He therefore describes the heart of the Christian story as "the absolute paradox," meaning by this that the mysteriousness of the incarnation is not something relative to human intelligence or education, as if those with theology degrees or high IQs could understand it while lesser mortals would have to be content with faith.

One might well think that this paradoxicality would make faith impossible, but Kierkegaard denies that this is the case. In fact, he claims that on reflection we can see that this paradox is precisely what we should expect in a true revelation from God, a sign of the "correctness" of the hypothesis that God has become human.[4] Contrary to what we might think, the paradoxicality supports the truth of the Christian story, even though Kierkegaard acknowledges the off-putting nature of the claim as well. (I will say more about this off-putting nature below.)

To help us understand all this, in his book *Philosophical Fragments* Kierkegaard draws an extended analogy between the Christian story of the incarnation and a love affair between an absolute monarch and a peasant.[5] Imagine that a mighty king

4. Kierkegaard, *Philosophical Fragments*, 22.
5. What follows is taken loosely from ibid., chap. 2. Strictly speaking, *Philosophical Fragments* is attributed by Kierkegaard to a pseudonymous character he has invented, Johannes Climacus, and thus what I am going to describe should really be attributed to this character. However, we know that Kierkegaard wrote *Philosophical Fragments* under his own name originally; the pseudonym was inserted at the last minute after the

has fallen in love with a humble maiden. How can the king achieve union with the woman? Kierkegaard himself believes that no true love is possible without mutual understanding and thus successful communication.[6] This creates problems for the king.

If he woos her as the king, how can he be assured that she understands his love and loves him freely in return? After all, as the king he could simply order her to marry him or else be thrown into the dungeon, but such coerced love would hardly satisfy the king. Another alternative might be to have the king bring the maiden to the palace and dazzle her with his riches, buying exquisite clothes for her and throwing magnificent balls. However, this possibility brings with it a worry that the woman would not really love the king but only the riches. Somehow the king must communicate his love for the young woman in such a way that she has the strength and independence to love him freely in return.

We all know what the king must do. In the fairy tale he must come in disguise, appearing to be a simple peasant himself so as to woo his love. This method is risky. Unlike the other possibilities he has rejected, the king understands that she may reject him. She may not understand him, and even if he lets her know who he really is, she may not grasp why he has behaved in this way. It is a risk the king must run; only in this way can he communicate his love so that she can love him in return.

Kierkegaard himself stresses that the analogy between this story and the incarnation is imperfect. One important difference is that when God comes to us in human form, the humanity is

book was in proofs. Moreover, it is easy to see from a comparison of this book with other nonpseudonymous works of Kierkegaard that Kierkegaard was fully in agreement with his created character on these issues. For scholarly purposes it is important to take the pseudonym seriously, as I do in my commentary on *Philosophical Fragments*. Readers who are interested in these issues are referred to that commentary, *Passionate Reason*.

6. Kierkegaard, *Philosophical Fragments*, 25–26.

not merely a disguise; rather, God fully embraces our human condition. Nevertheless, the analogy helps us understand why God might reveal himself in this way. If God simply reveals himself as the almighty and all-knowing one, we humans might well be intimidated by his power or seduced by what he can do for us. Only by coming to us "incognito" can God show us that his love is the deepest and most important element in his nature. He demonstrates his love for us by sharing in our situation, including our sufferings and even death. At the same time he allows us the freedom to respond (or not respond) to that love. As Kierkegaard affirms, God knows that by acting in this way he risks being spurned by us, but it is the only way he can develop a relationship of love with us. As I have already said, Kierkegaard affirms that the story is one that humans are likely to find off-putting, and he believes God understands this too. Nevertheless God sees it as the only way he can accomplish his goal.

Why is it the case that we are likely to find the story off-putting? I discussed this issue briefly in the last chapter, but it is important enough to reiterate and expand on the main points. Kierkegaard affirms that the ground of what he calls the "offense" found in the story lies in human sinfulness.[7] We can understand this if we look at the way sin manifests itself in humans. The problem of sin chiefly lies in the fact that we humans are dominated by pride and selfishness. Once we understand this, we can easily see how these characteristics make it hard for us to believe the story.

Let us first consider pride. The incarnation is something human reason finds deeply mysterious, something we cannot fully understand. Actually, a person who really knows and trusts God will not find this to be a problem. After all, God is God, and we humans are finite creatures. Why should we expect to

7. Ibid., 47.

be able to understand all that God can do? However, if we are dominated by pride, we will likely be tempted to make our own understanding the measure of what is possible. In effect we put ourselves in the place of God and say that what we cannot understand is impossible. The incarnation is "absurd," the "strangest possible thing," or the "most improbable thing of all."[8]

The second element of sinfulness is selfishness. We humans are not completely self-centered. We are capable of caring about others and sometimes doing what is best for others. Even when we do this, however, we are probably never completely free from self-centered motives. We are willing to help others, but we want them (and others) to recognize our magnanimity and give us the credit we deserve. When others say they want to help us and be our benefactors, we are naturally suspicious. We wonder what is in it for them.

This makes it difficult for us to believe the story of the incarnation, for that story is a story of completely unselfish love. God does not need humans at all. He does not need our love or our worship to be complete. The Christian God does not even need humans in order to be loving, because the Christian God is a Trinity, three persons who love one another perfectly for all eternity. God's love for humans is not motivated by need of any kind; it is simply a kind of overflow of the love of the Trinity itself. Since we humans have no experience of such love apart from God's love for us in Christ, we naturally find it hard to believe this really happened.

It follows from this that when human reason denounces the Christian story as absurd or impossible, reason is not a neutral spectator, simply looking at the evidence dispassionately. Rather, reason is a passionate reason, shaped by its pride and selfishness. Kierkegaard thinks that people of faith should not be surprised by this reaction. In fact, when one thinks about

8. Ibid., 52, 101.

it in the right way, this negative reaction is itself a sign of the genuineness of the revelation. It shows that the story is indeed one that no human would have made up.[9] The offended reaction of the unbeliever is actually further confirmation of the truth of the incarnation.

But how is it possible for humans to come to believe the story? The answer is that those sinful passions must be supplanted by a new passion: the passion of faith. When God offers his love to humans in Christ, that love can transform the person. If the person is willing to recognize the limits of human thinking by admitting the pride and selfishness that shape that thinking, then everything looks different. The fact that we cannot understand how God could do this seems perfectly right, for we are not God. Why should we expect to understand God's ways? The love that God offers us shows us how selfish we are but also the possibility of a new way of living. Faith is thus God's gift, something God creates in a person when that person encounters God in Jesus Christ.

Existential Power

It should be clear that in speaking about the criterion of paradoxicality we have already been speaking about the third criterion: the existential power of the revelation. Remember that the paradoxicality is only an initial paradoxicality. When the individual has experienced the life-transforming power of God's revelation, the story begins to seem like the only one that really makes sense. It is a story that tells me who I am and also who I can become. And it offers me a path toward becoming that true self. When I turn to God in faith I discover God's church, Christ's body, a community through which God continues Christ's work in my life.

9. Ibid., 35–36.

Of course, the criterion of existential power is a very personal criterion. Kierkegaard recognized this by saying that the deepest truths cannot be communicated directly from one human to another; rather, they can only be communicated through what he called "indirect communication." In the end I can only offer my human testimony to the power of God as I have experienced God in Christ and extend to others an invitation to "taste and see that the Lord is good" (Ps. 34:8).

Bibliography

Aquinas, Thomas. *Summa Contra Gentiles*. Book I. Translated by Anton C. Pegis. Notre Dame, IN: University of Notre Dame Press, 1991.

———. *Summa Theologica*. 5 vols. New York: Benziger Bros., 1948.

Augustine. *Confessions*. 2nd ed. Translated by F. J. Sheed. Edited by Michael P. Foley. Indianapolis: Hackett, 2006.

Barrett, Justin. *Why Would Anyone Believe in God?* Cognitive Science of Religion. Walnut Creek, CA: Altamira, 2004.

Barth, Karl. *Natural Theology: Comprising "Nature and Grace" and the Reply "No."* Edited by G. Bles. London: Centenary, 1946.

Boyer, Pascal. *The Naturalness of Religious Ideas: A Cognitive Theory of Religion*. Berkeley: University of California Press, 1994.

Bultmann, Rudolf. *Kerygma and Myth*. New York: Harper and Row, 1961.

Butler, Joseph. *Analogy of Religion*. New York: E. P. Dutton, 1906.

Buxani, Silvan D. *Salam: Divine Revelations from the Actual God*. New York: SAU Salam Foundation, 2003.

Camus, Albert. *The Myth of Sisyphus and Other Essays*. New York: Random House, 1955.

Chesterton, G. K. *Orthodoxy*. Garden City, NY: Doubleday, 1959.

Collins, Francis. *The Language of God: A Scientist Presents Evidence for Belief*. New York: Free Press, 2006.

Craig, William Lane. *Historical Evidence for the Resurrection of Jesus*. Eugene, OR: Wipf and Stock, 2000.

Dawkins, Richard. *The Blind Watchmaker: Why the Evidence of Evolution Reveals a Universe without Design*. New York: W. W. Norton, 1986.

———. *The God Delusion*. Boston: Houghton Mifflin, 2006.

———. *The Selfish Gene*. 2nd ed. Oxford: Oxford University Press, 1998.

Dennett, Daniel C. *Brainstorms: Philosophical Essays on Mind and Psychology*. Montgomery, VT: Bradford, 1978.

———. *Breaking the Spell: Religion as a Natural Phenomenon*. New York: Viking, 2006.

———. *Consciousness Explained*. Boston: Little, Brown, 1991.

———. *Darwin's Dangerous Idea: Evolution and the Meanings of Life*. New York: Touchstone, 1995.

———. *The Intentional Stance*. Cambridge, MA: MIT Press, 1987.

Dennett, Daniel C., and Alvin Plantinga. *Science and Religion: Are They Compatible?* Oxford: Oxford University Press, 2011.

Dworkin, Ronald. *Justice for Hedgehogs*. Cambridge, MA: Harvard University Press, 2011.

———. "What Is a Good Life?" *New York Review of Books* 58, no. 2 (February 10, 2011): 41–43.

Evans, C. Stephen. "Canonicity, Apostolicity, and Biblical Authority: Some Kierkegaardian Reflections." In *Canon and Biblical Interpretation*, edited by Craig Bartholomew, Scott Hahn, Robin Parry, Christopher Seitz, and Al Wolters, 146–66. Grand Rapids: Zondervan, 2006.

———. *God and Moral Obligation*. Oxford: Oxford University Press, 2013.

———. *The Historical Christ and the Jesus of Faith: The Incarnational Narrative as History*. Oxford: Oxford University Press, 1996.

———. "Kierkegaard on Religious Authority: The Problem of the Criterion." In *Kierkegaard on Faith and the Self*, 239–62. Waco: Baylor University Press, 2006.

———. *Kierkegaard's Ethic of Love: Divine Commands and Moral Obligations*. Oxford: Oxford University Press, 2004.

———. *Kierkegaard's* Fragments *and* Postscript*: The Religious Philosophy of Johannes Climacus*. 1983. Reprint, Amherst, NY: Humanity Books, 1999.

———. *Natural Signs and Knowledge of God: A New Look at Theistic Arguments*. Oxford: Oxford University Press, 2010.

———. *Passionate Reason: Making Sense of Kierkegaard's* Philosophical Fragments. Bloomington: Indiana University Press, 1992.

———. *Why Believe? Reason and Mystery as Pointers to God*. Grand Rapids: Eerdmans, 1996.

Evans, C. Stephen, and R. Zachary Manis. *Philosophy of Religion: Thinking about Faith*. 2nd ed. Downers Grove, IL: InterVarsity, 2009.

Evans, Jan. *Miguel de Unamuno's Quest for Faith: A Kierkegaardian Understanding of Unamuno's Struggle to Believe*. Eugene, OR: Pickwick, 2013.

Flew, Antony. *The Presumption of Atheism and Other Essays on God, Freedom, and Immortality*. London: Pemberton, 1976.

Flew, Antony, and Roy Abraham Varghese. *There Is a God: How the World's Most Notorious Atheist Changed His Mind*. New York: HarperCollins, 2008.

Harris, Sam. *The End of Faith: Religion, Terror, and the Future of Reason*. New York: W. W. Norton, 2005.

———. *Free Will*. New York: Free Press, 2012.

———. *Letter to a Christian Nation*. New York: Alfred A. Knopf, 2006.

———. *The Moral Landscape: How Science Can Determine Human Values*. New York: Free Press, 2010.

Hitchens, Christopher. *God Is Not Great: How Religion Poisons Everything*. New York: Twelve, 2007.

Hume, David. *Dialogues concerning Natural Religion*. Edited by Richard H. Popkin. Indianapolis: Hackett, 1980.

———. *An Enquiry concerning Human Understanding*. Indianapolis: Hackett, 1993.

Jackson, Timothy P. *The Priority of Love: Christian Charity and Social Justice*. Princeton: Princeton University Press, 2003.

Kant, Immanuel. *Critique of Pure Reason*. Translated by Norman Kemp Smith. New York: St. Martin's Press, 1965.

Keener, Craig S. *Miracles: The Credibility of the New Testament Accounts*. 2 vols. Grand Rapids: Baker Academic, 2011.

Kelemen, Deborah. "Are Children 'Intuitive Theists'? Reasoning about Purpose and Design in Nature." *Psychological Science* 15 (2004): 295–96.

Kierkegaard, Søren. *Philosophical Fragments*. Translated and edited by Edna H. Hong and Howard V. Hong. Princeton: Princeton University Press, 1985.

———. *Søren Kierkegaard's Journals and Papers*. Vol. 1. Translated and edited by Edna H. Hong and Howard V. Hong. Bloomington: Indiana University Press, 1967.

———. *Without Authority*. Translated and edited by Howard V. Hong and Edna H. Hong. Princeton: Princeton University Press, 1997.

———. *Works of Love*. Edited and translated by Howard V. Hong and Edna H. Hong. Kierkegaard's Writings. Princeton: Princeton University Press, 1995.

Kuhn, Thomas. *The Structure of Scientific Revolutions*. Chicago: University of Chicago Press, 1970.

Lewis, C. S. *Mere Christianity*. London: Collins, 1952.

———. *Miracles*. San Francisco: HarperOne, 2001.

———. *Surprised by Joy: The Shape of My Early Life*. London: Geoffrey Bles, 1955.

———. "The Weight of Glory." In *The Weight of Glory and Other Addresses*, 25–36. New York: Macmillan, 1980.

Locke, John. *An Essay concerning Human Understanding*. Kitchener, ON: Batoche, 2001.

Mackie, J. L. *Ethics: Inventing Right and Wrong*. London: Penguin, 1977.

McDonald, Lee Martin. *The Formation of the Christian Biblical Canon*. Peabody, MA: Hendrickson, 1995.

Moser, Paul K. "Cognitive Idolatry and Divine Hiding." In *Divine Hiddenness*, edited by D. Howard-Snyder and Paul Moser, 120–48. New York: Cambridge University Press, 2002.

———. "Death, Dying, and the Hiddenness of God." In *The Philosophy of Religion Reader*, edited by Chad Meister, 613–24. London: Routledge, 2008.

———. *The Elusive God: Reorienting Religious Epistemology*. Cambridge: Cambridge University Press, 2008.

Neill, Stephen, and N. T. Wright. *The Interpretation of the New Testament, 1861–1986*. 2nd ed. Oxford: Oxford University Press, 1988.

Paley, William. *A View of the Evidences of Christianity*. New York: Robert Carter and Bros., 1854.

Pascal, Blaise. *Pensées*. New York: E. P. Dutton, 1958.

Peterson, Michael, ed. *The Problem of Evil: Selected Readings*. Notre Dame, IN: University of Notre Dame Press, 1992.

Plantinga, Alvin. "Reason and Belief in God." In *Faith and Rationality: Reason and Belief in God*, edited by Alvin Plantinga and Nicholas Wolterstorff, 16–93. Notre Dame, IN: University of Notre Dame Press, 1983.

————. *Warranted Christian Belief.* New York: Oxford University Press, 2000.

————. "What Is 'Intervention'?" *Theology and Science* 6, no. 4 (2008): 369–401.

————. *Where the Conflict Really Lies: Science, Religion, and Naturalism.* Oxford: Oxford University Press, 2011.

Polkinghorne, John. *Belief in God in an Age of Science.* New Haven: Yale University Press, 1998.

Rowe, William. "The Evidential Argument from Evil: A Second Look." In *The Evidential Argument from Evil,* edited by Daniel Howard-Snyder, 262–85. Bloomington: Indiana University Press, 1996.

Russell, Jeffrey Burton. *Exposing Myths about Christianity: A Guide to Answering 145 Viral Lies and Legends.* Downers Grove, IL: InterVarsity, 2012.

Smart, J. J. C. *Our Place in the Universe: A Metaphysical Discussion.* Oxford: Blackwell, 1989.

Stark, Rodney. *The Victory of Reason: How Christianity Led to Freedom, Capitalism, and Western Success.* New York: Random House, 2005.

Swinburne, Richard. *The Christian God.* Oxford: Oxford University Press, 1994.

————. *The Concept of Miracle.* New York: Macmillan, 1971.

————. *The Existence of God.* 2nd ed. Oxford: Oxford University Press, 2004.

————. *Revelation: From Metaphor to Analogy.* Oxford: Oxford University Press, 1992.

Unamuno, Miguel de. "Diario intimo." In vol. 8 of *Obras completas* [Complete Works], edited by M. Garcia Blanco, 773–880. Madrid: Escelicer, 1966.

————. "Mi Religion." In vol. 3 of *Obras completas* [Complete Works], edited by M. Garcia Blanco, 259–63. Madrid: Escelicer, 1968.

Wolterstorff, Nicholas. *Journey toward Justice: Personal Encounters in the Global South.* Grand Rapids: Baker Academic, 2013.

————. *Justice: Rights and Wrongs.* Princeton: Princeton University Press, 2008.

Wright, N. T. *The Resurrection of the Son of God.* Christian Origins and the Question of God 3. Minneapolis: Fortress, 2003.

Index